ANIMAL KINGDOM

A Colouring Book
for relaxation and rejuvenation

Cassie Haywood

ISBN: 978-0-9944431-1-3

A CIP record for this book is available from the National Library of Australia

ANIMAL KINGDOM

Animals don't get caught up in worrying about what might happen next, so why should we? They eat, play, sleep and love unconditionally. We can learn so much from animals because they know how to 'be' in the world. Simply watching an animal can take you out of your mind and into the present moment, which is where animals live all the time, completely surrendered into life.

In this book you will find 50 illustrations inspired by the Animal Kingdom. Simply choose an animal which appeals to you, take a few deep breaths and start colouring. There are no rules to follow, you choose the medium and colours which speak to you. These illustrations open the way for letting go and inner peace, therefore allowing relaxation and rejuvenation to become part of your everyday life.

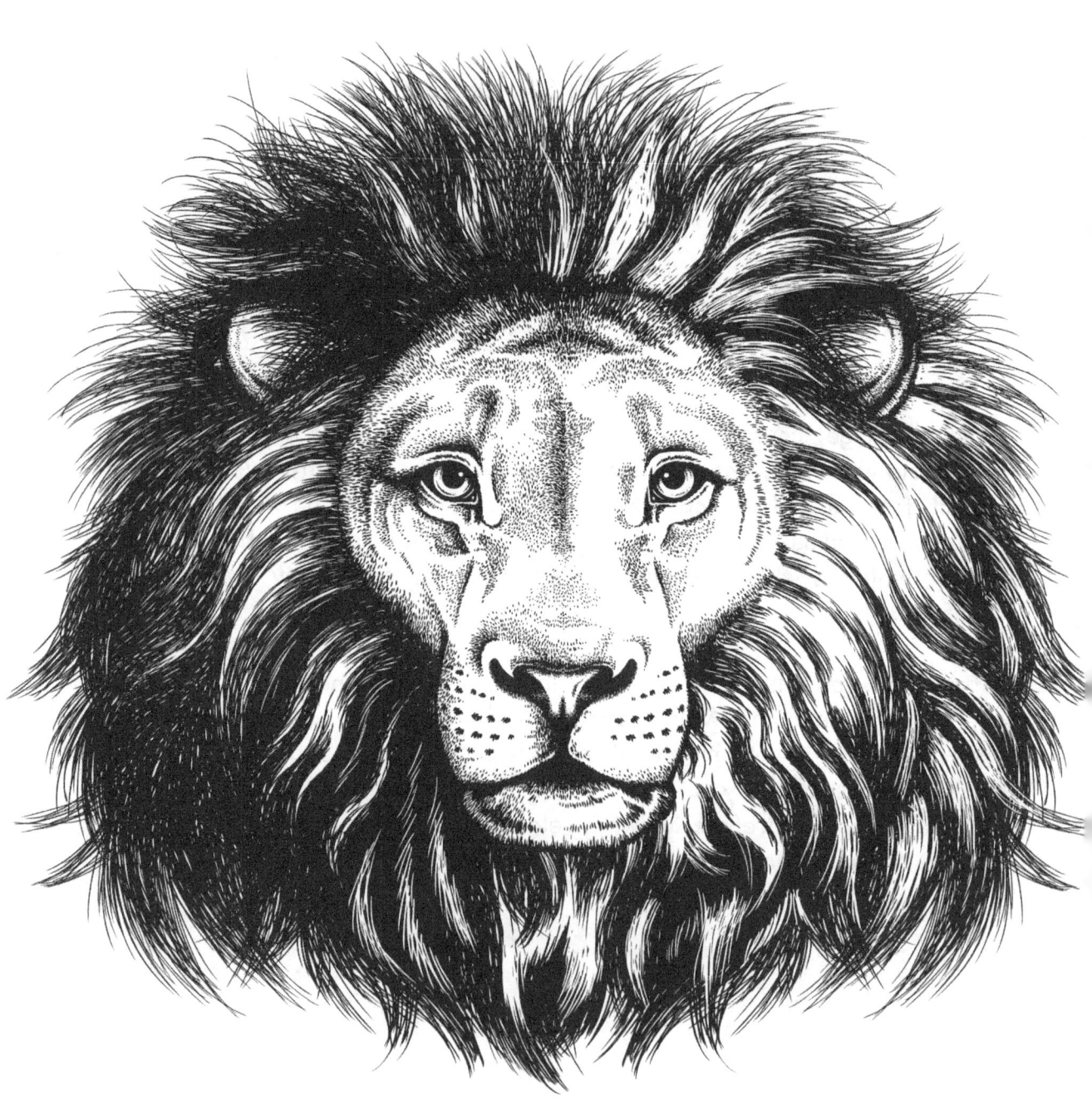

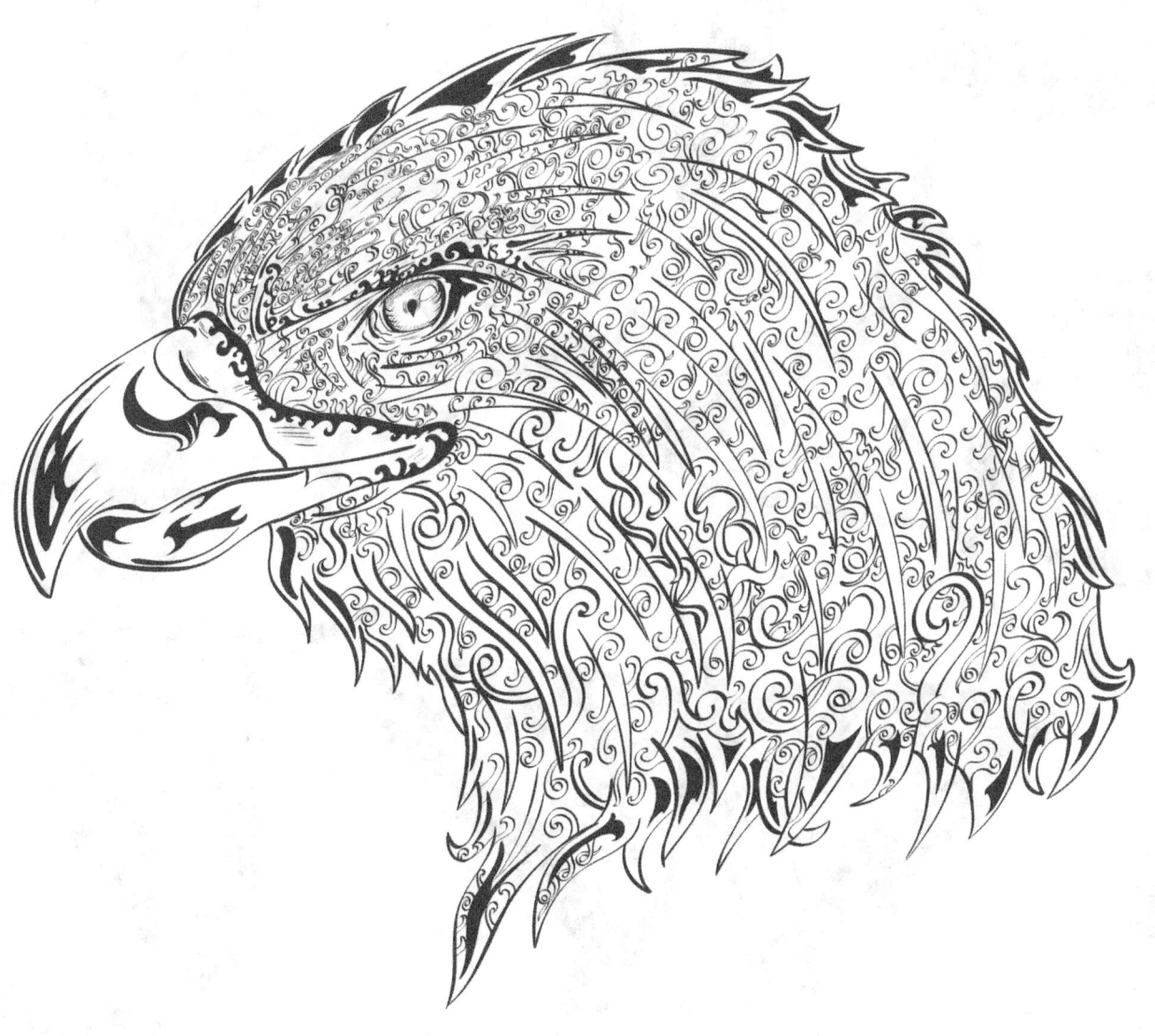

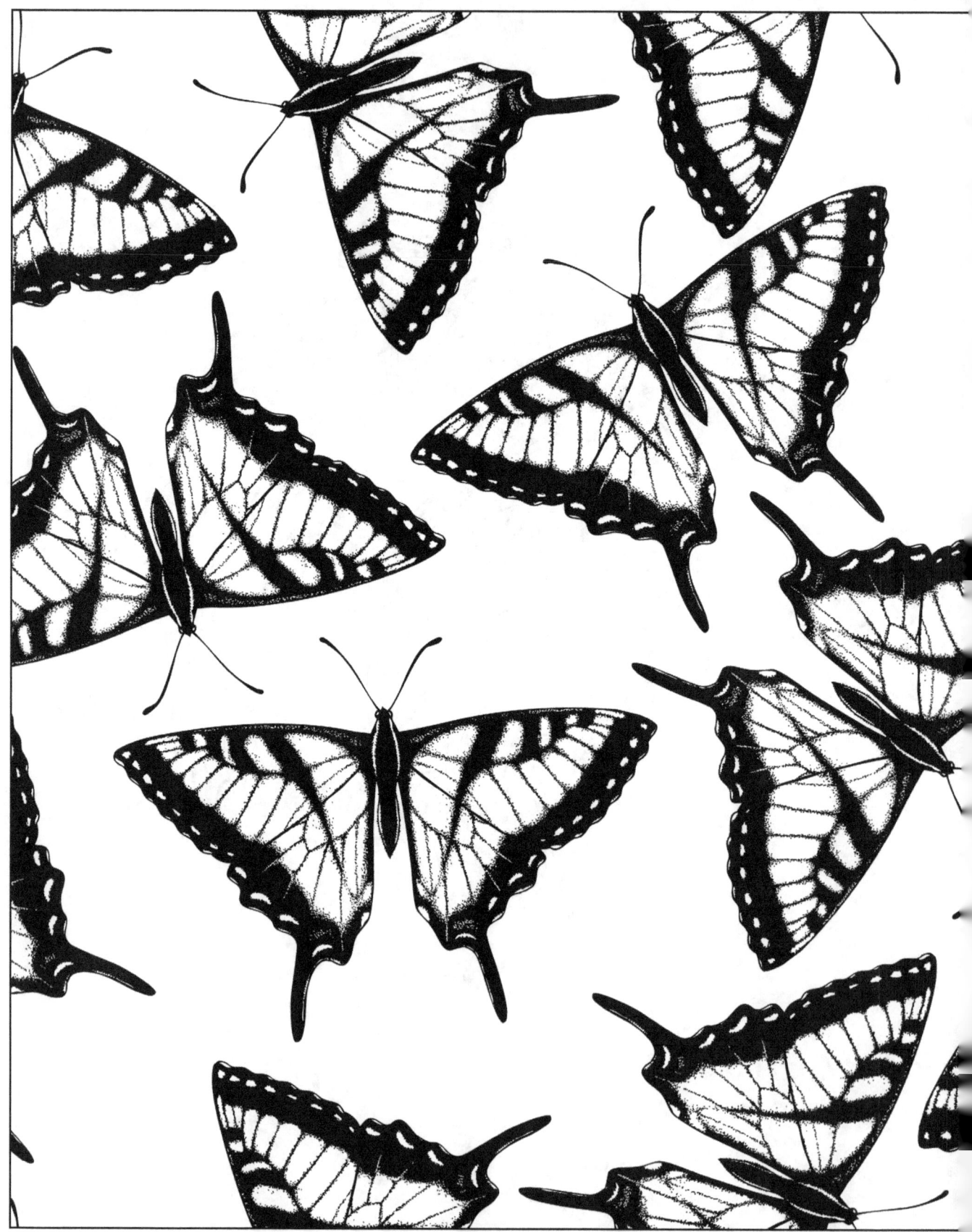

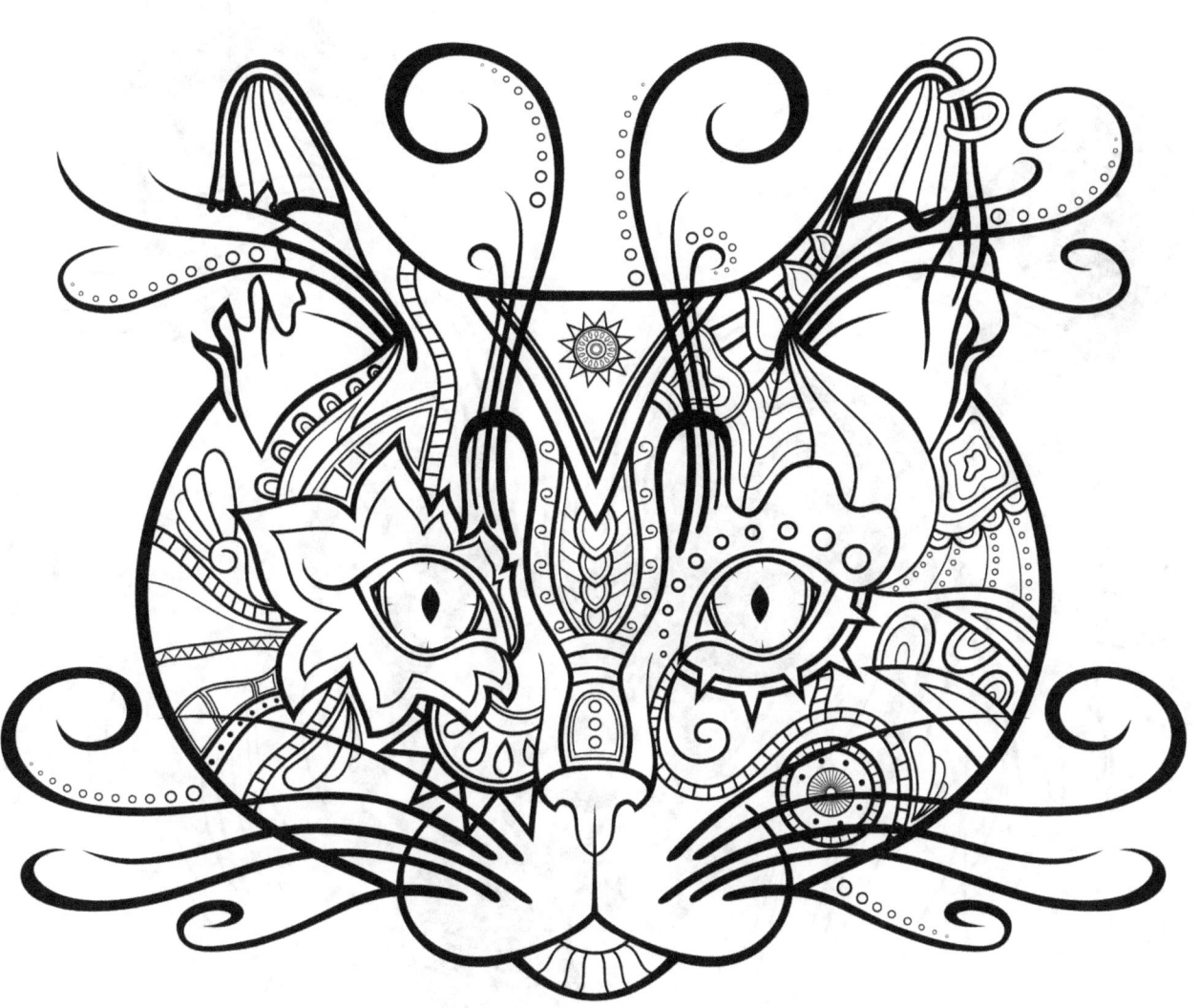

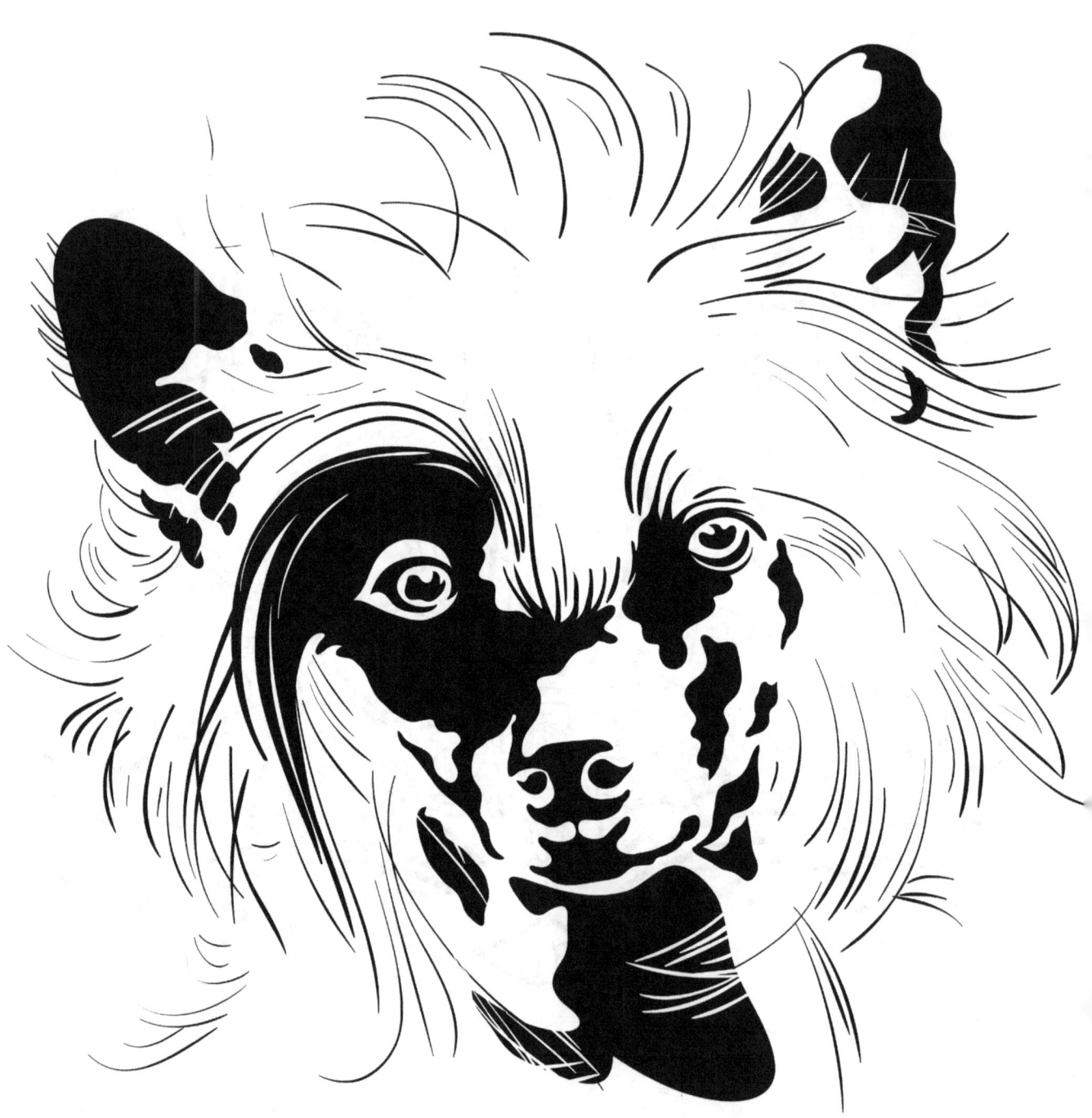

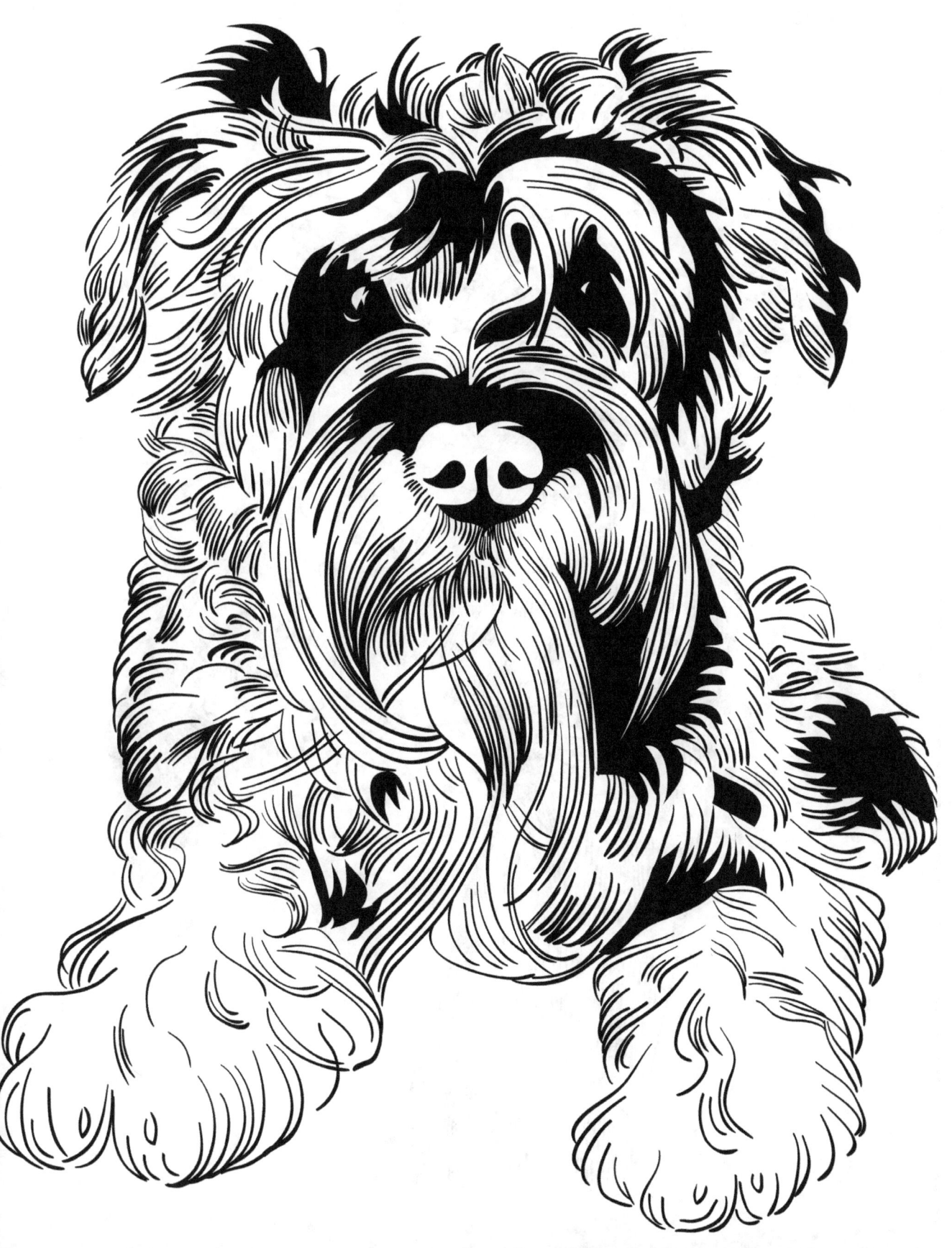

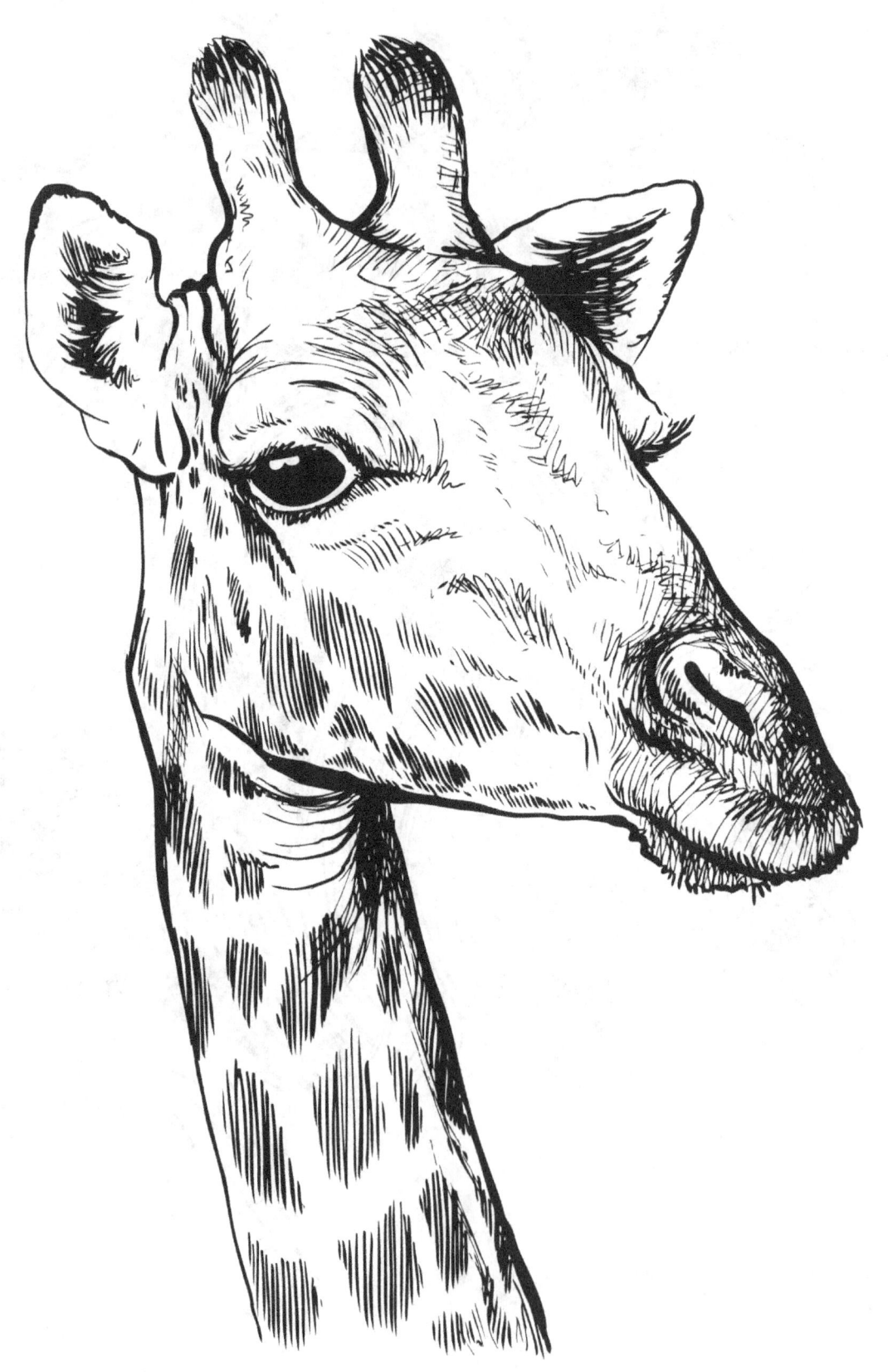

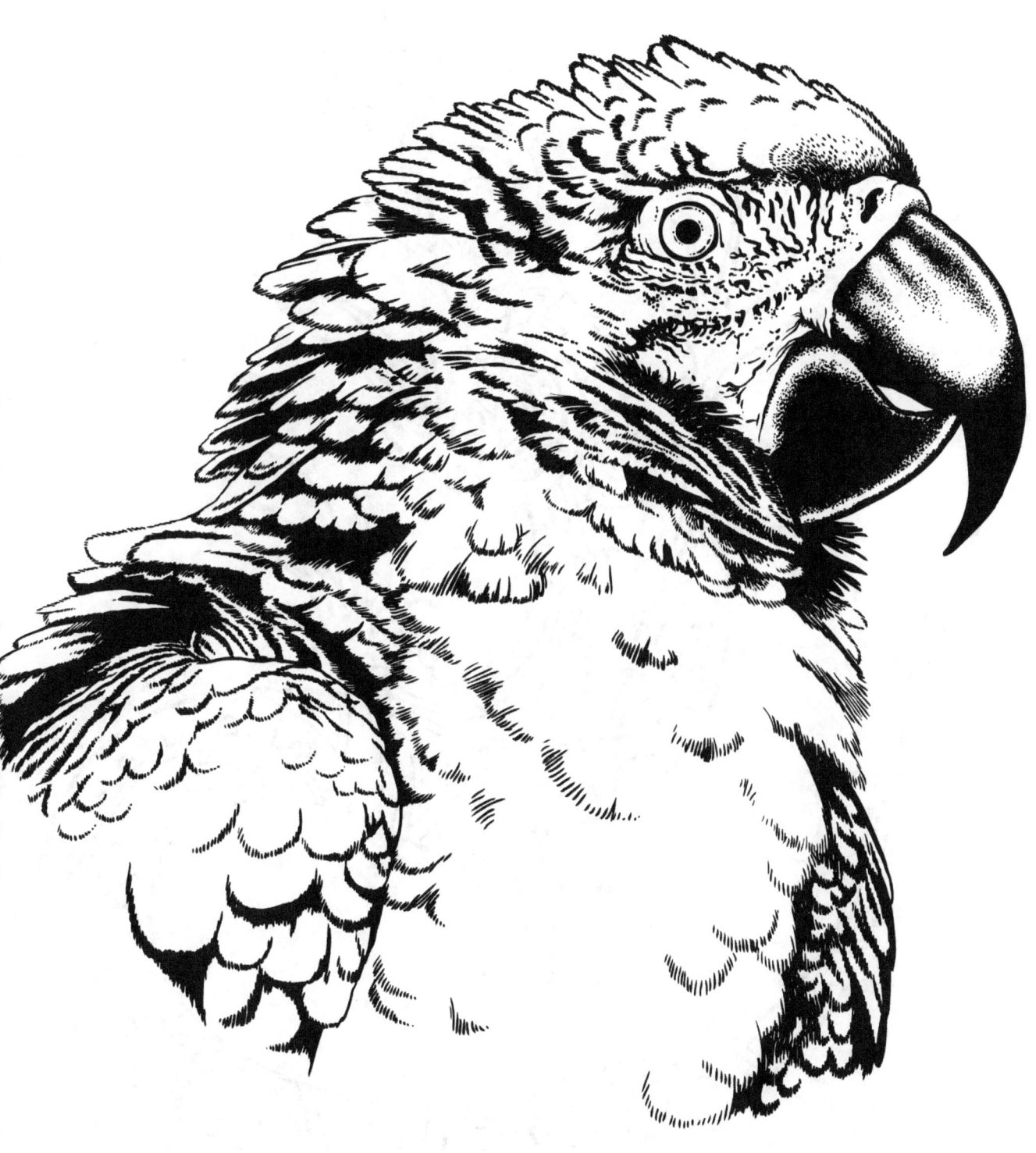

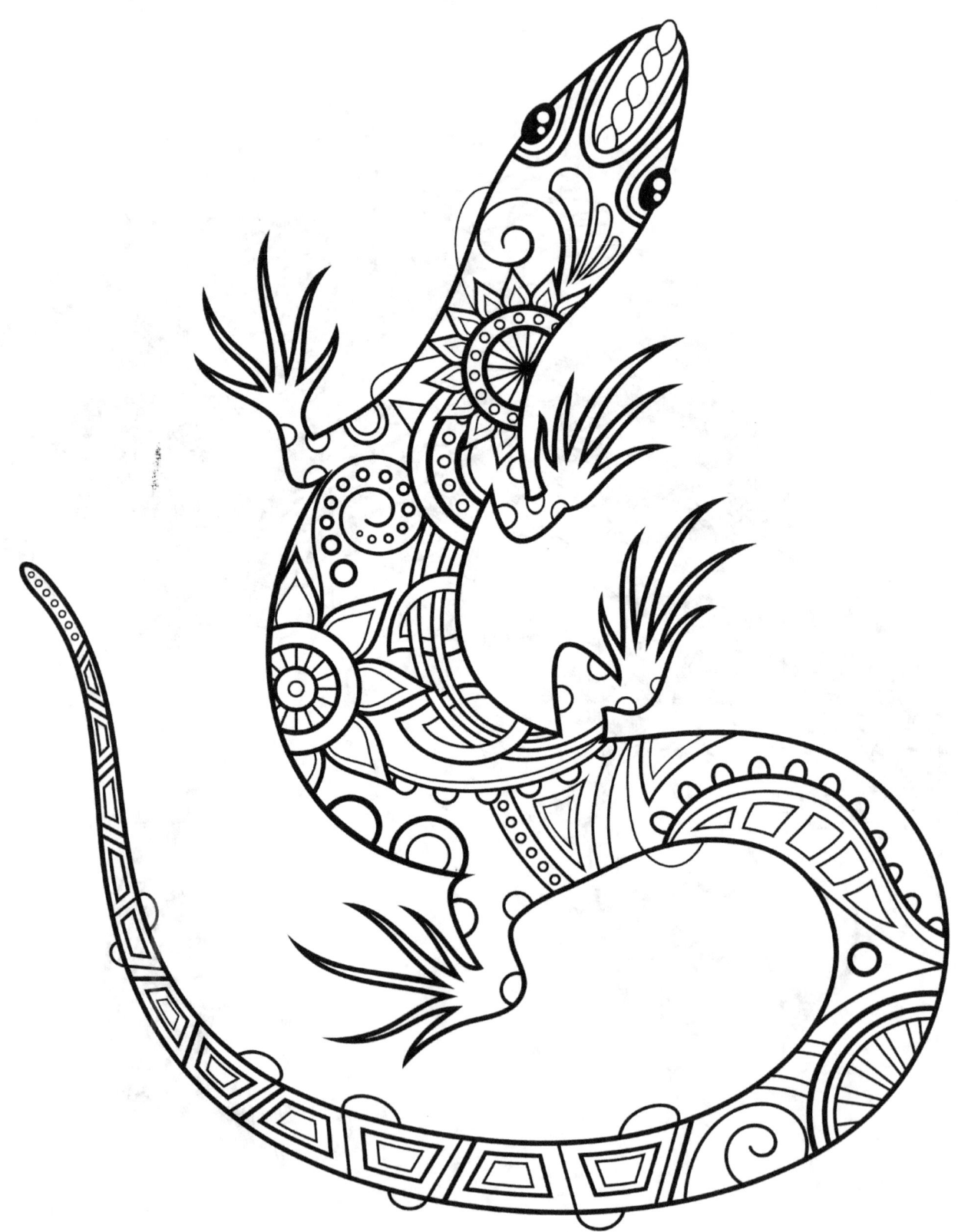

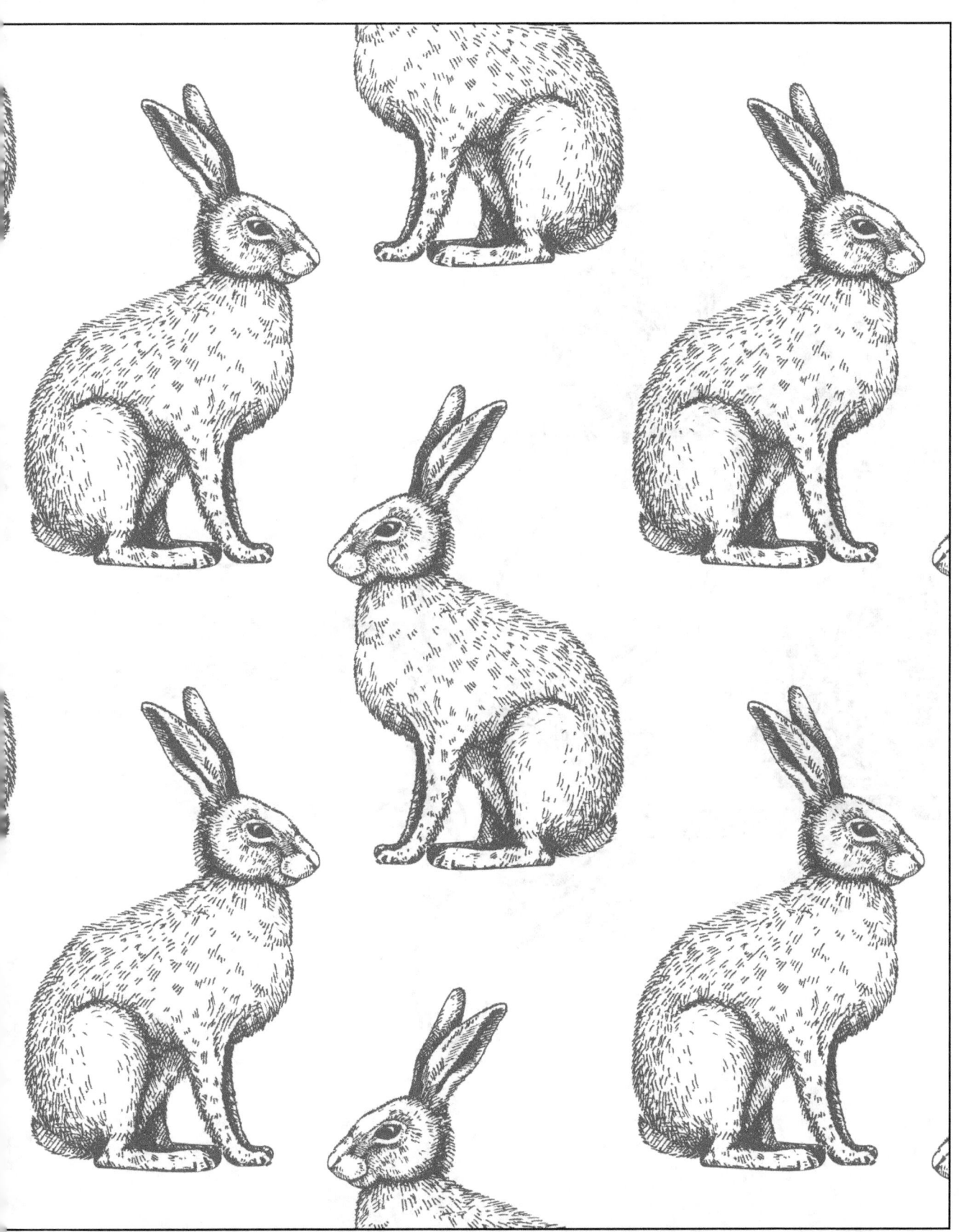

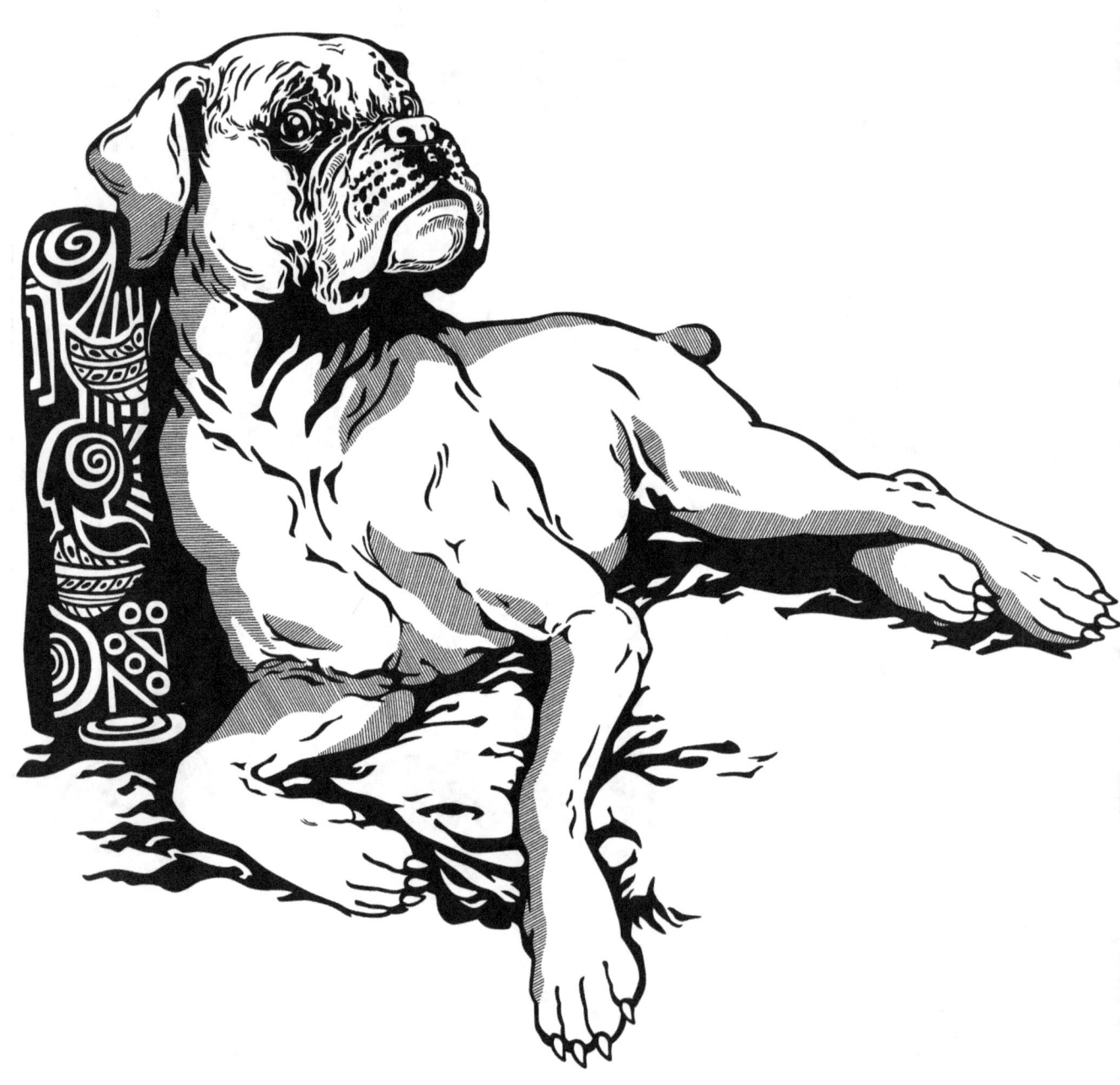

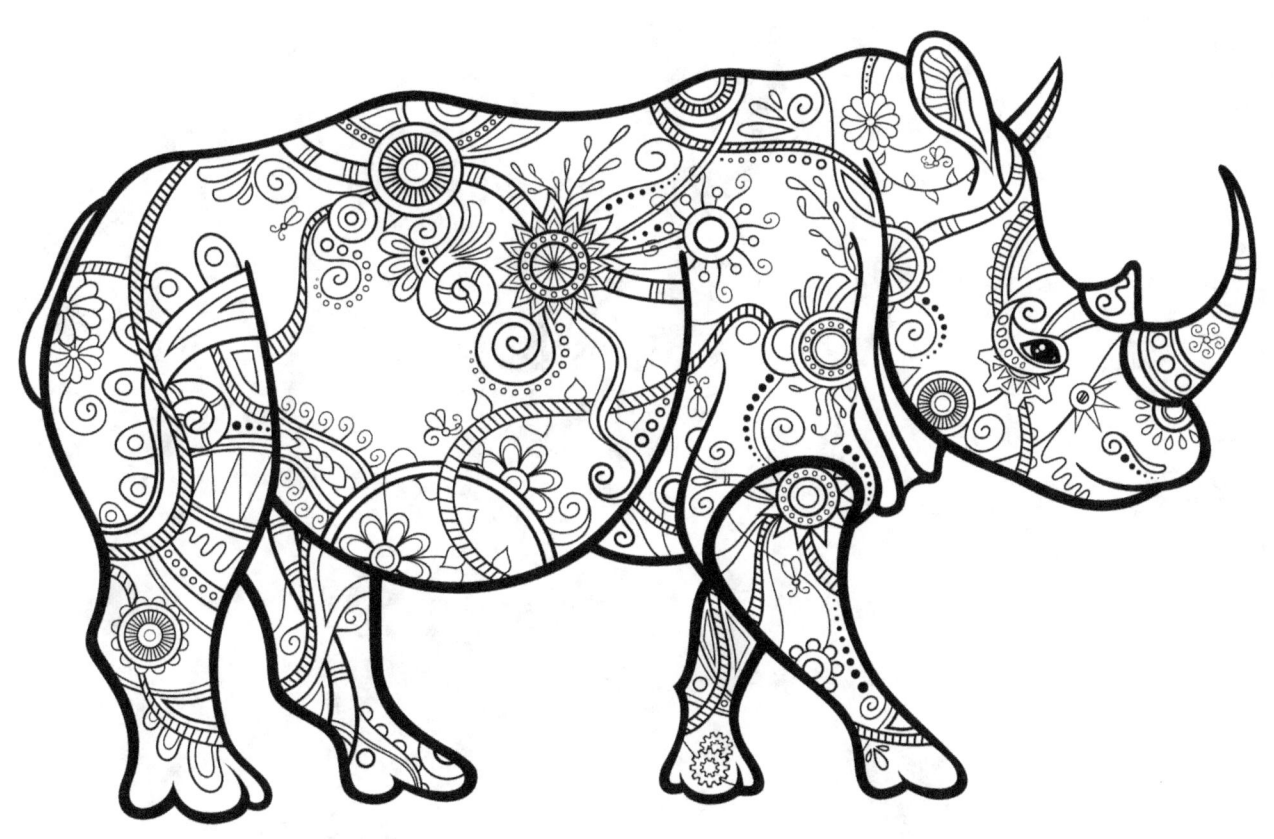

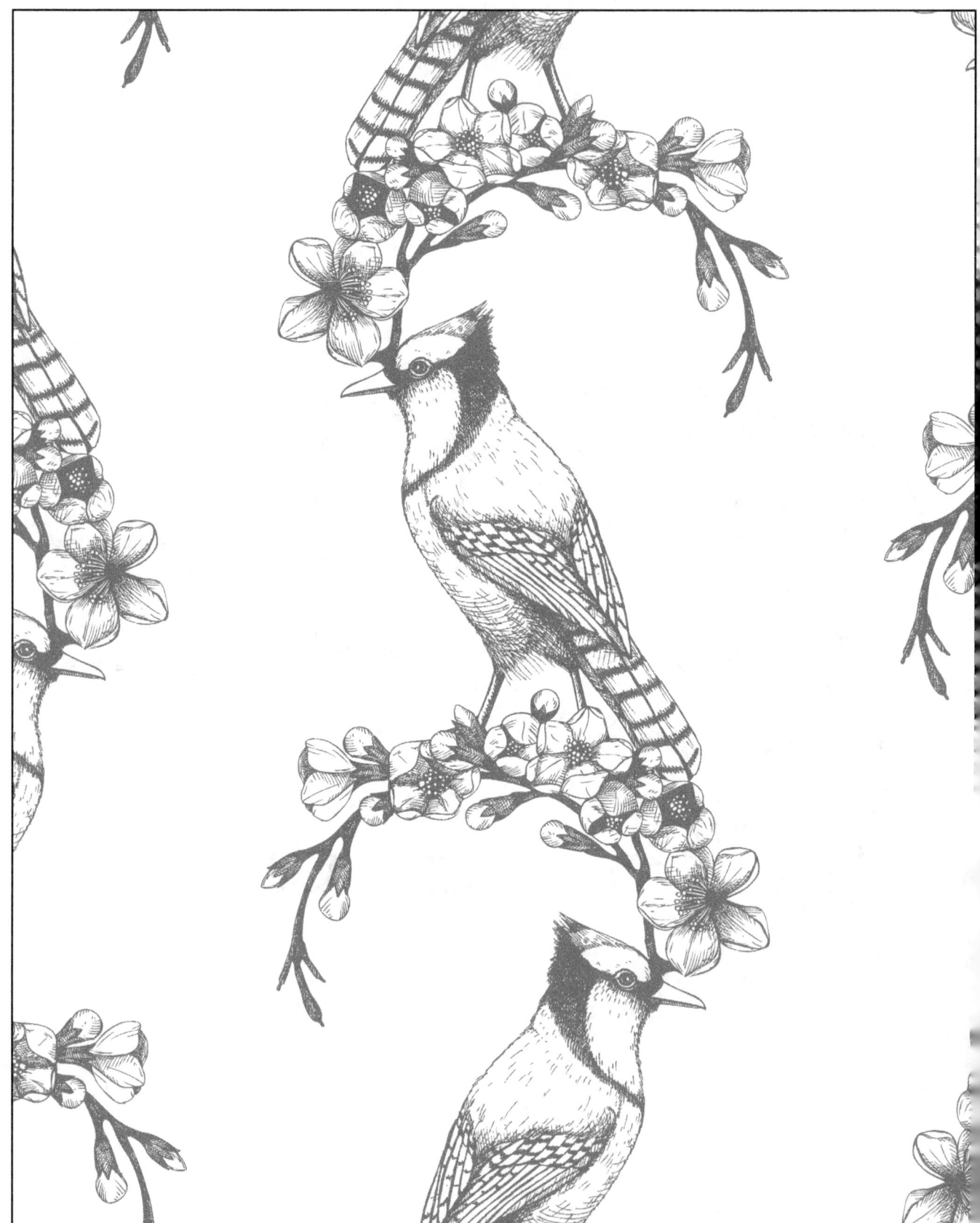

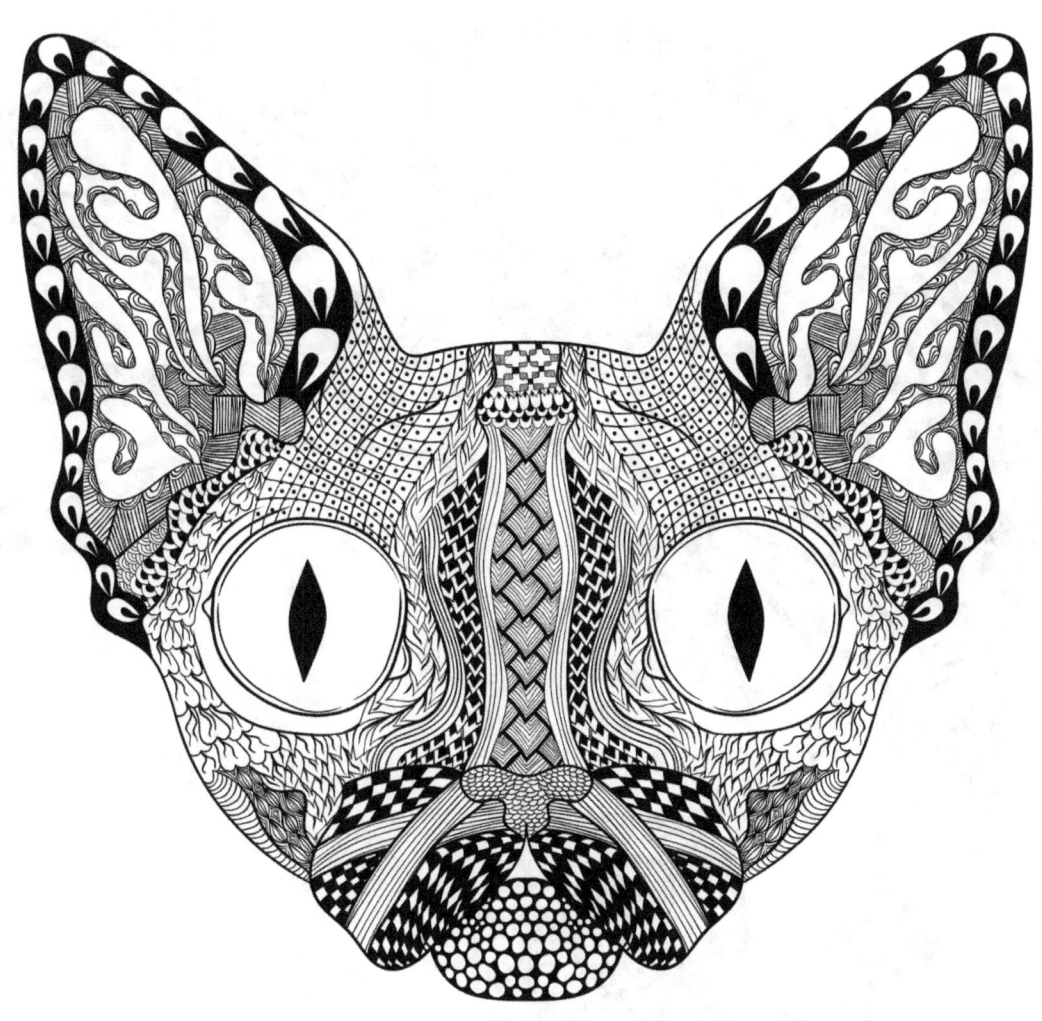

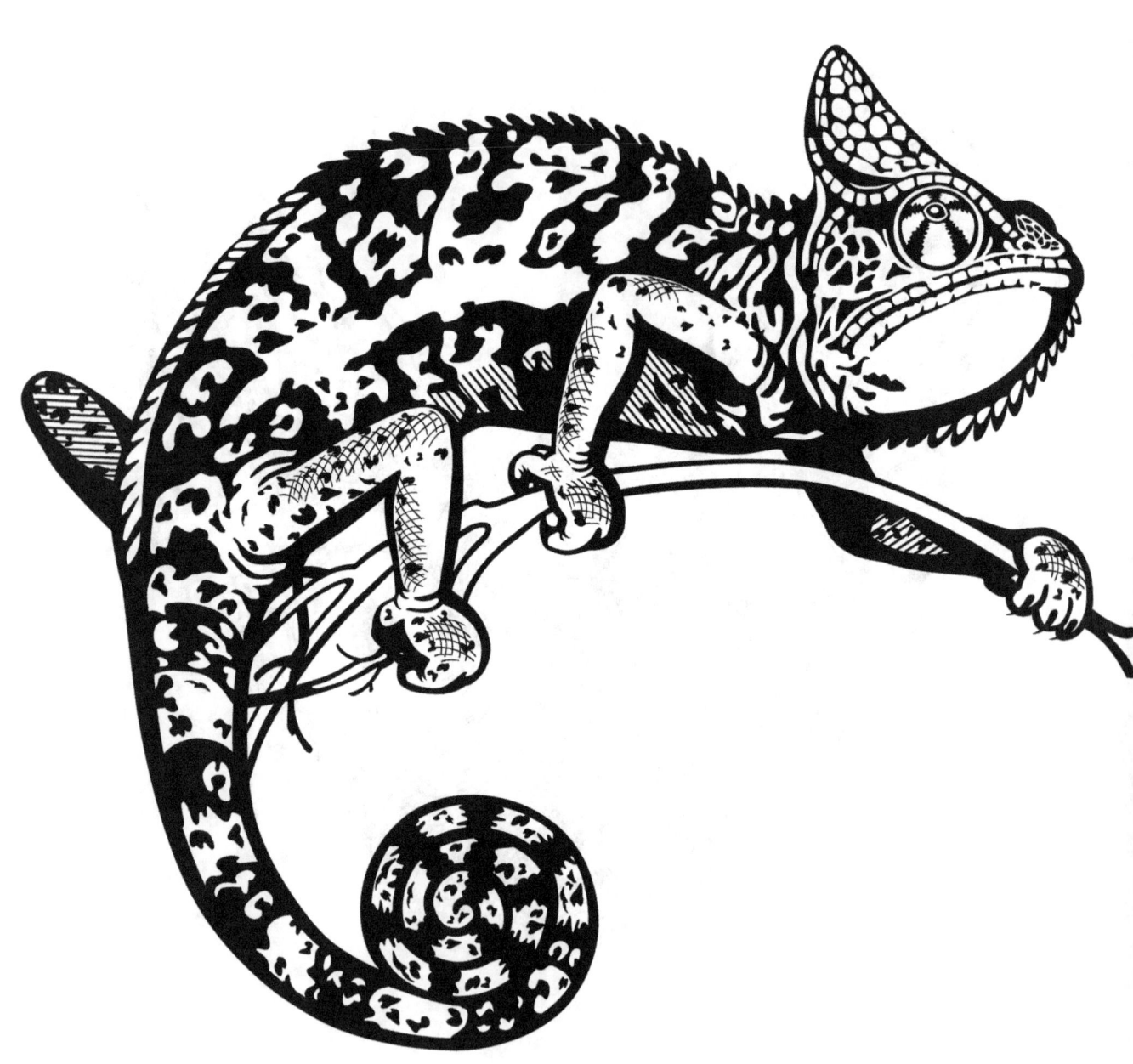

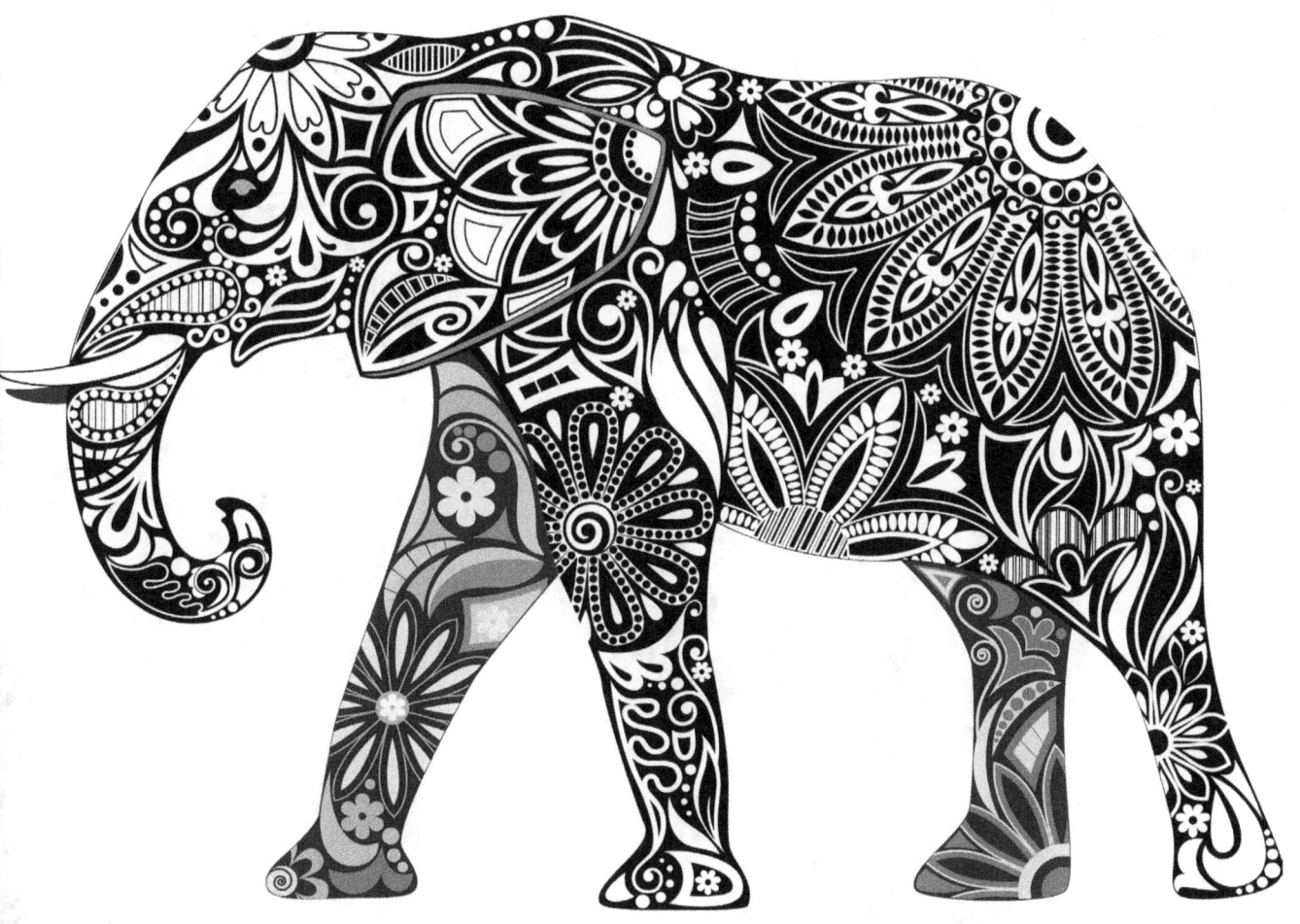

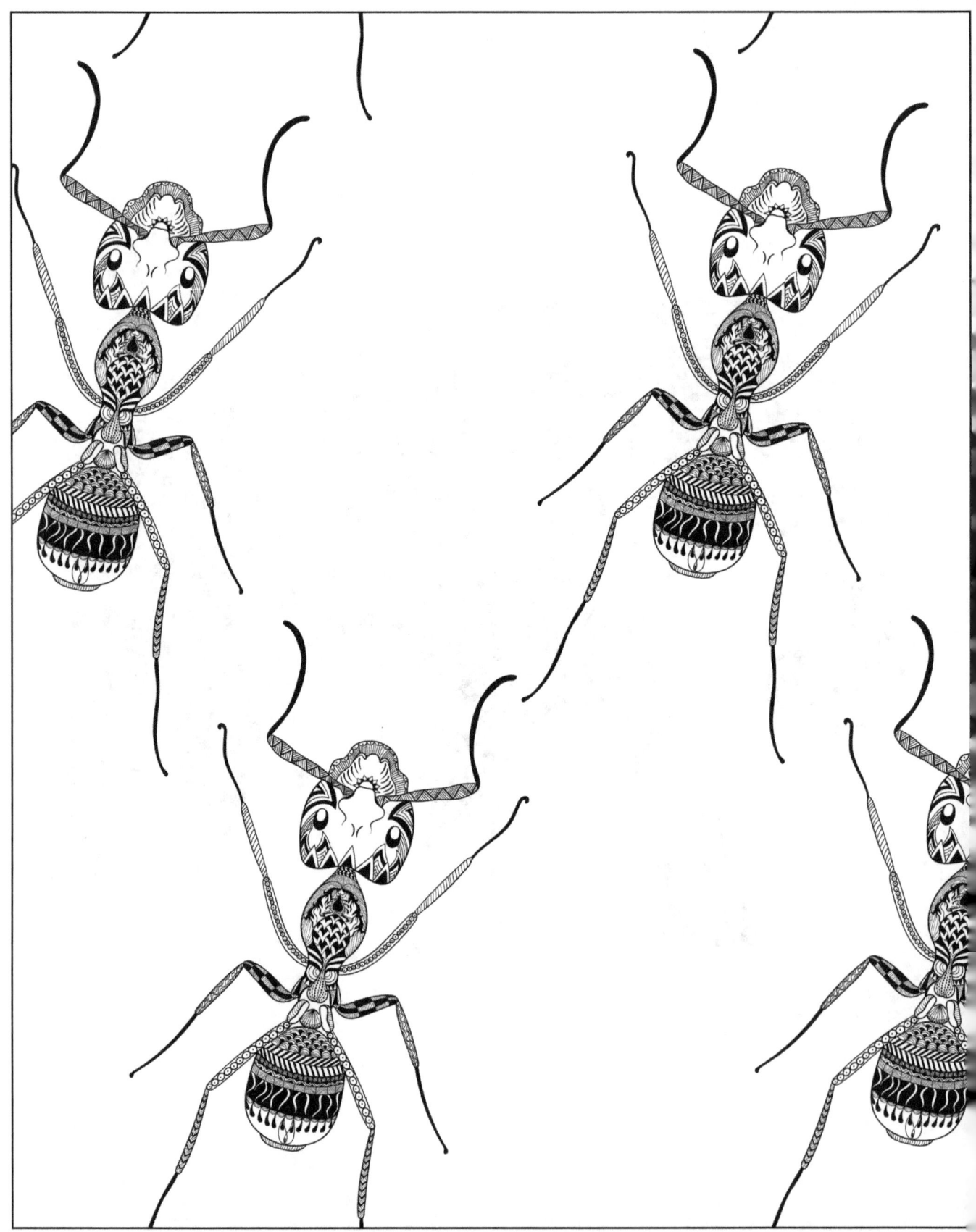

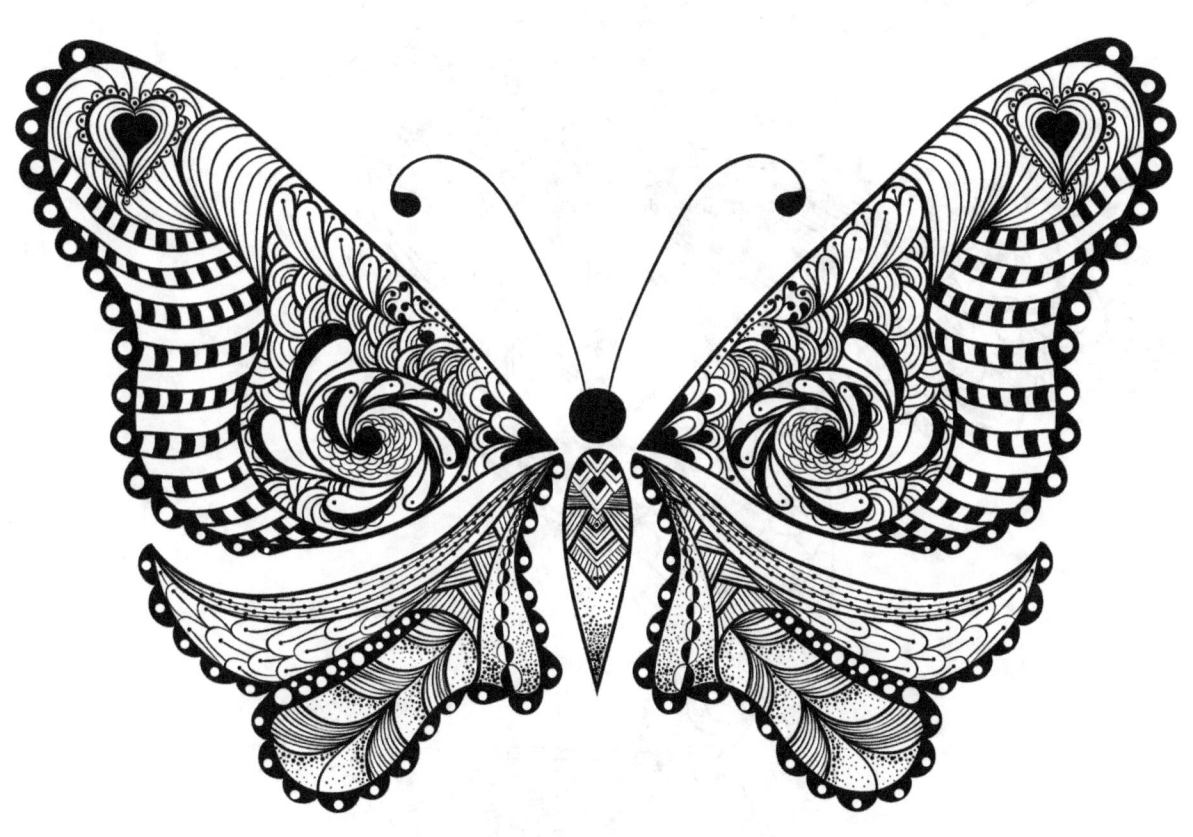

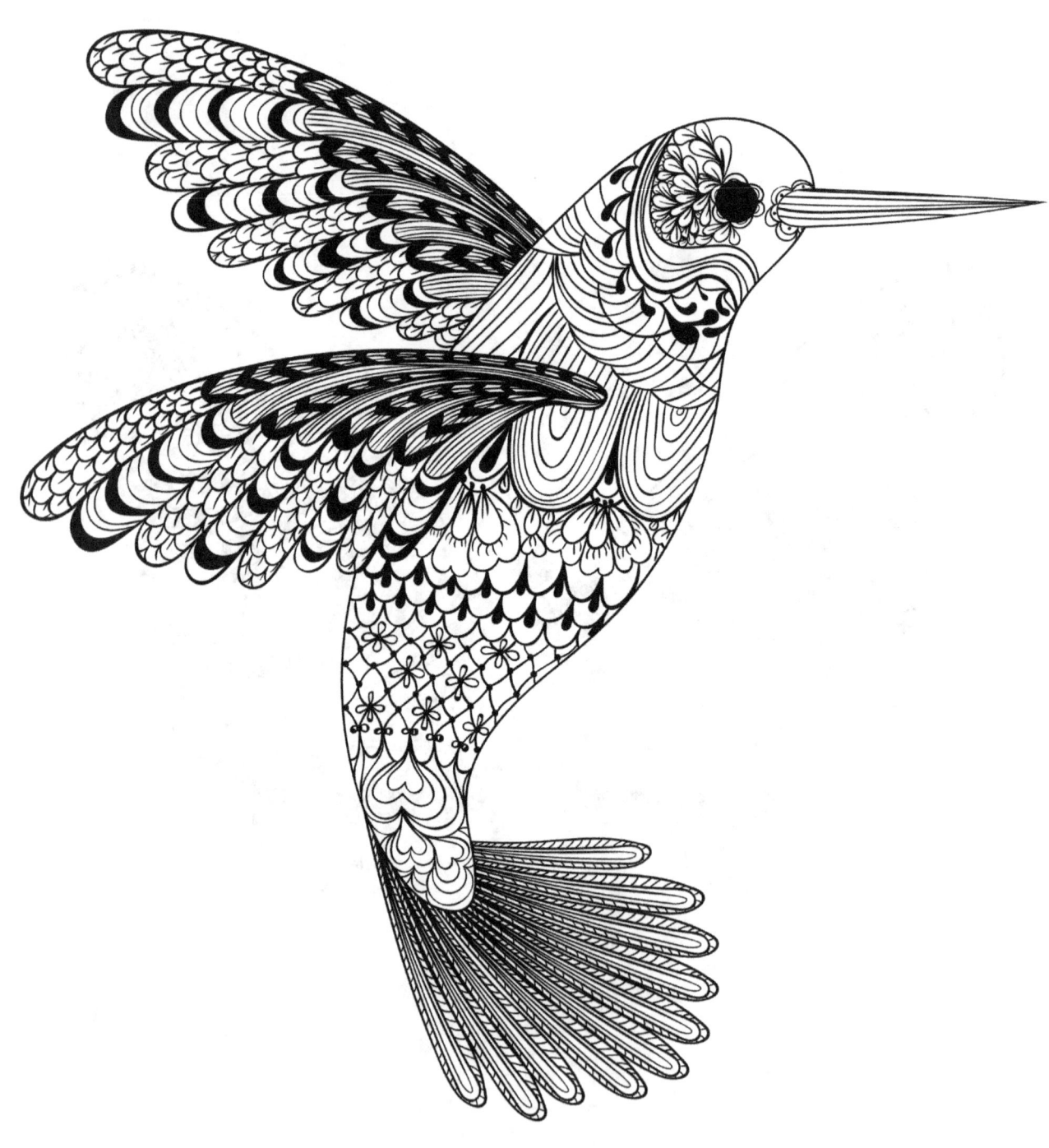

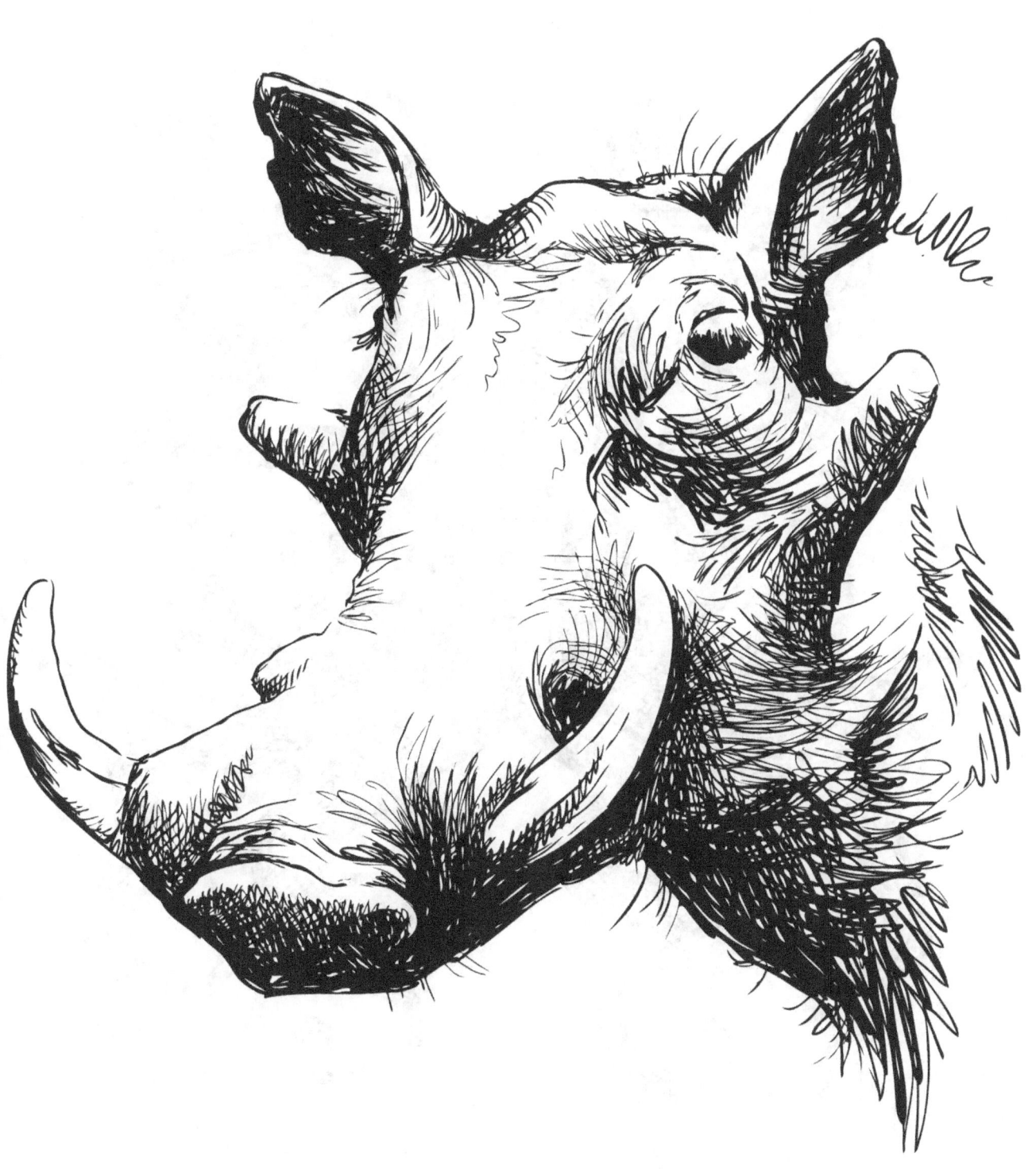

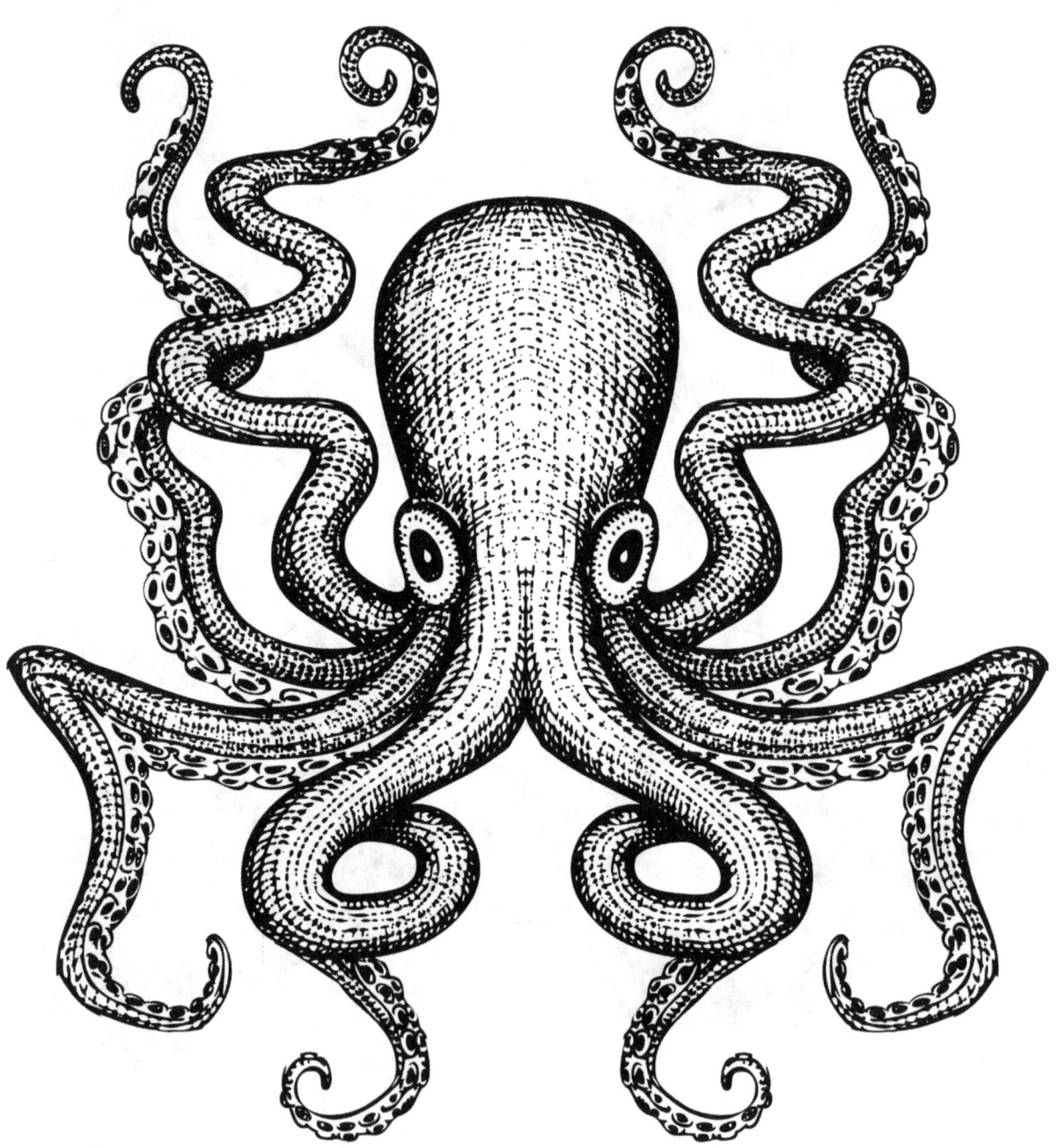

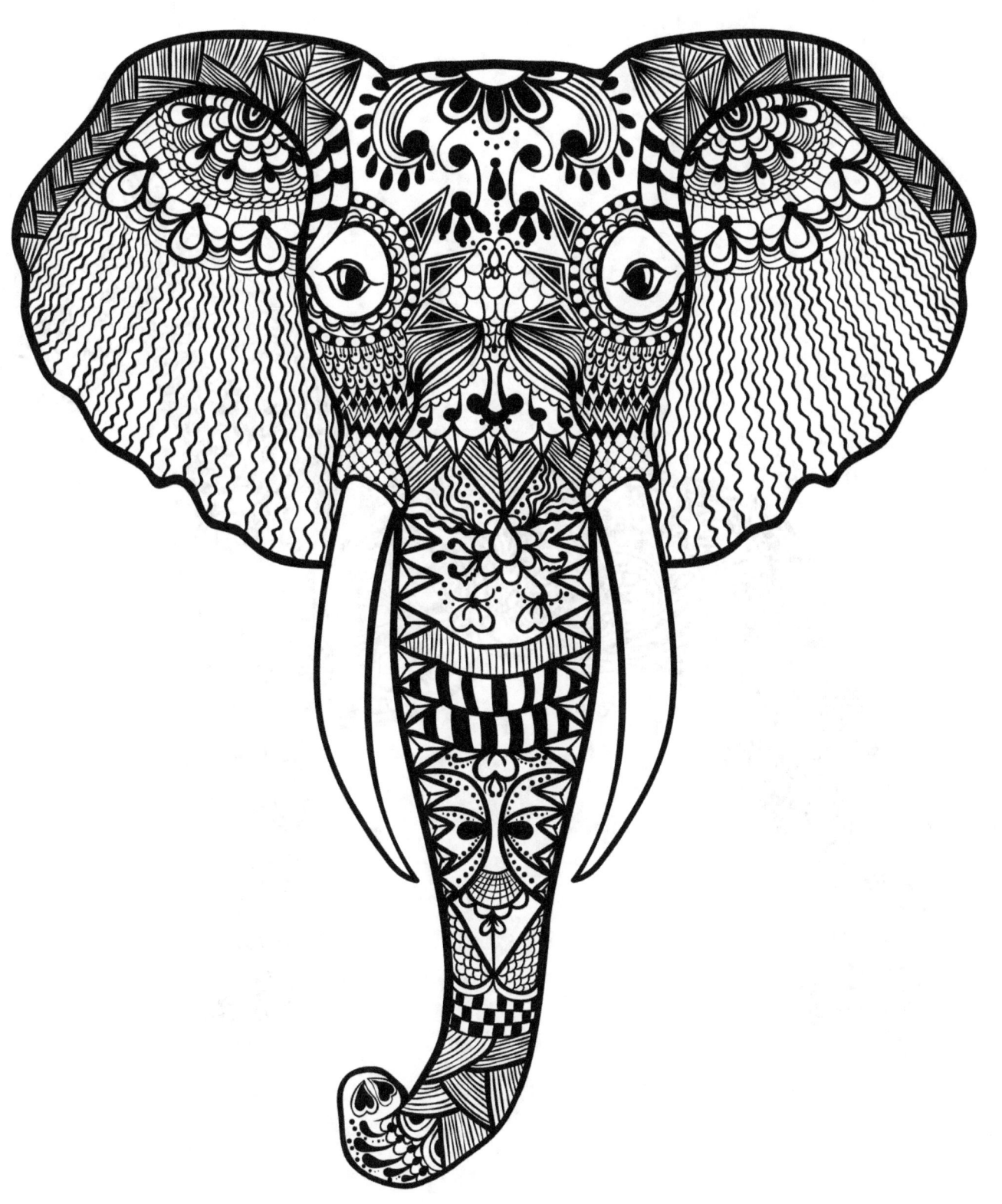

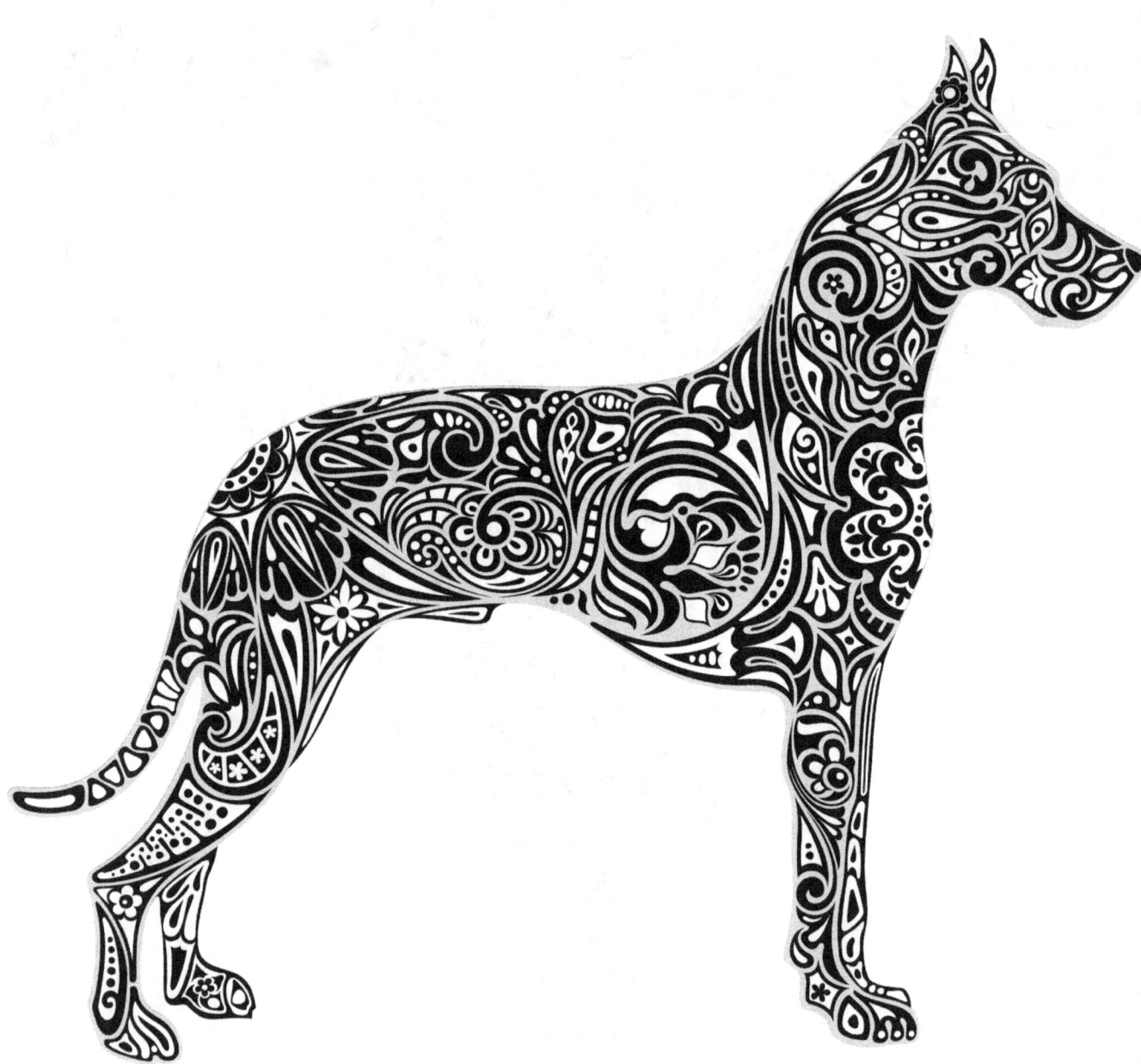

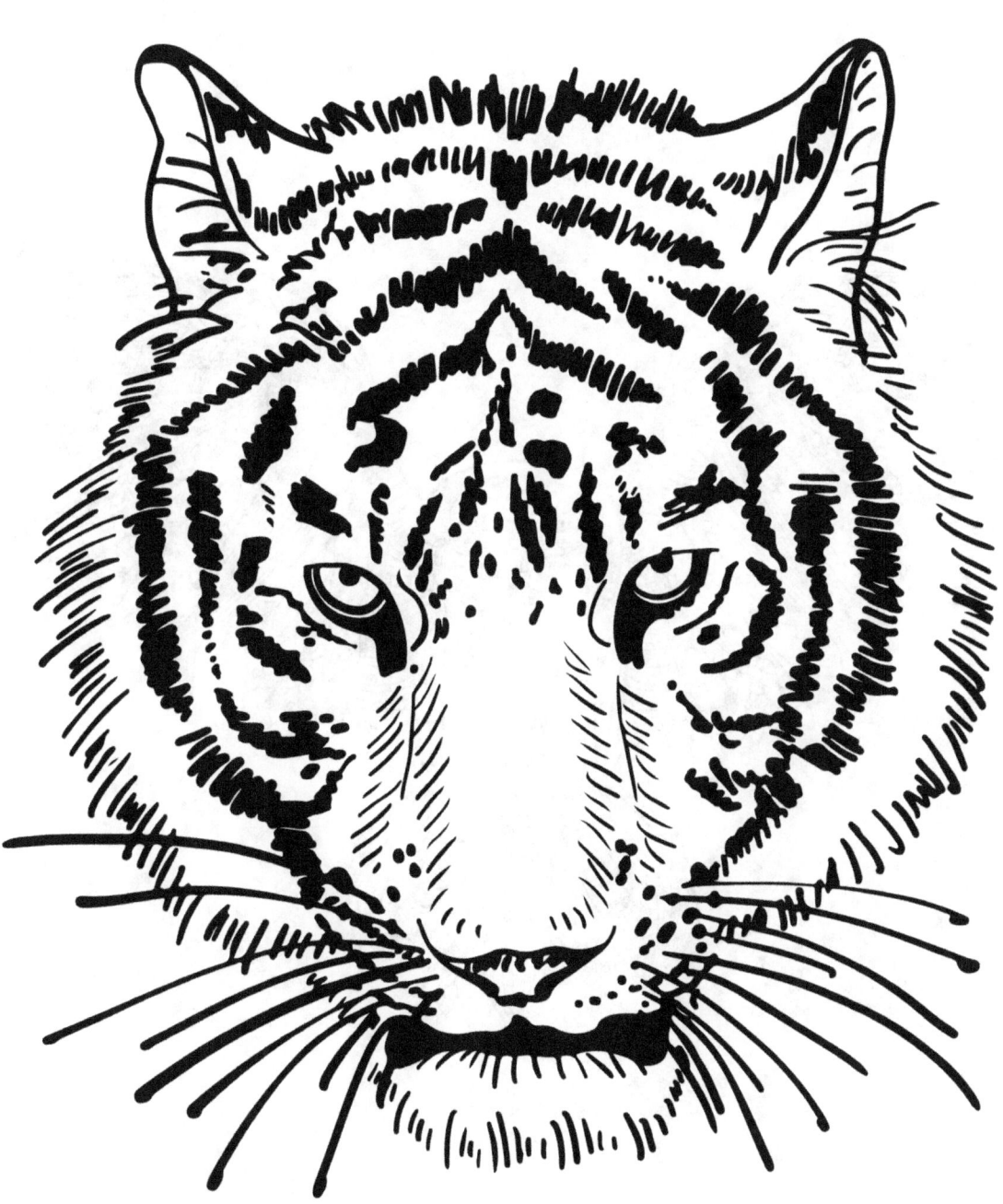

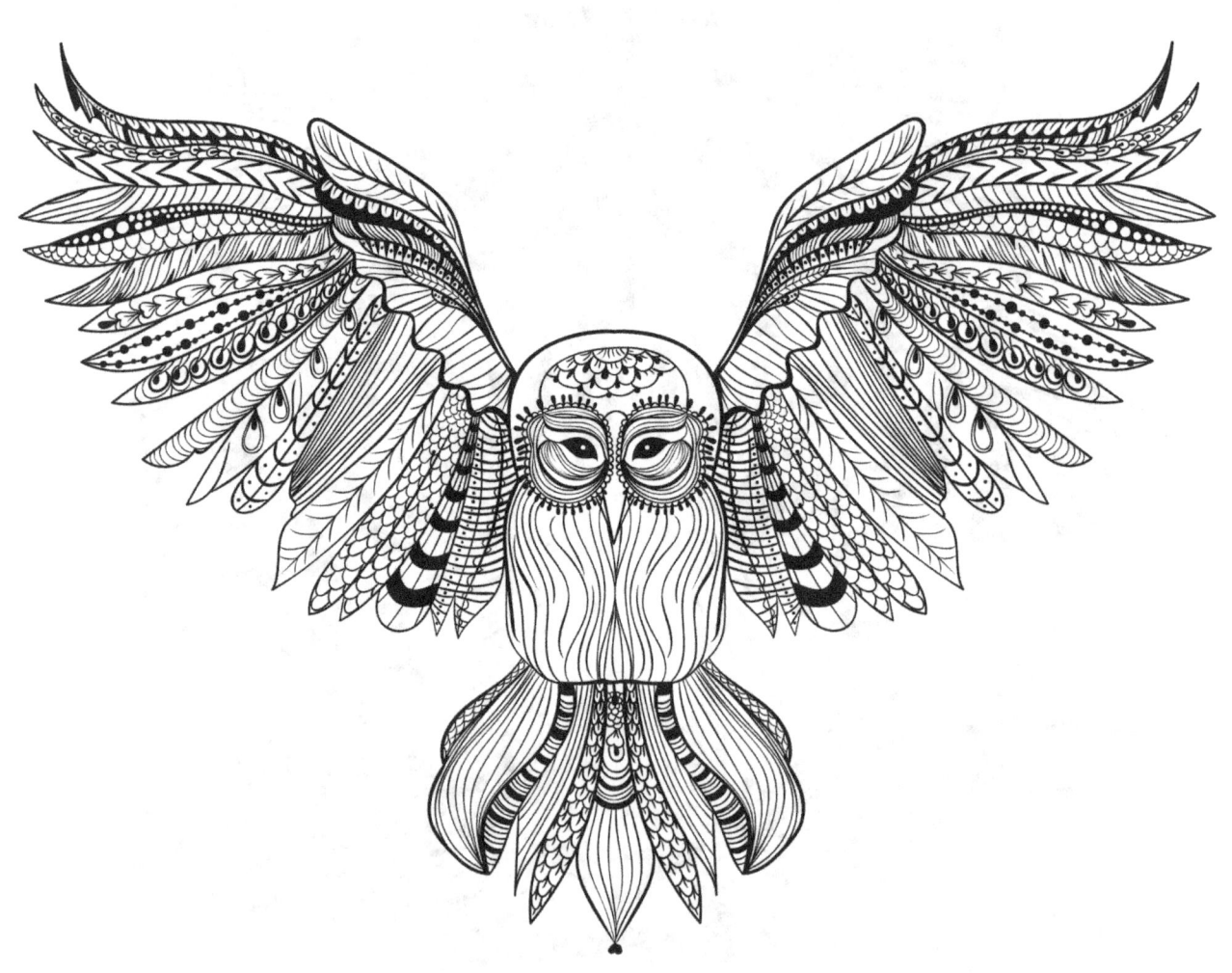

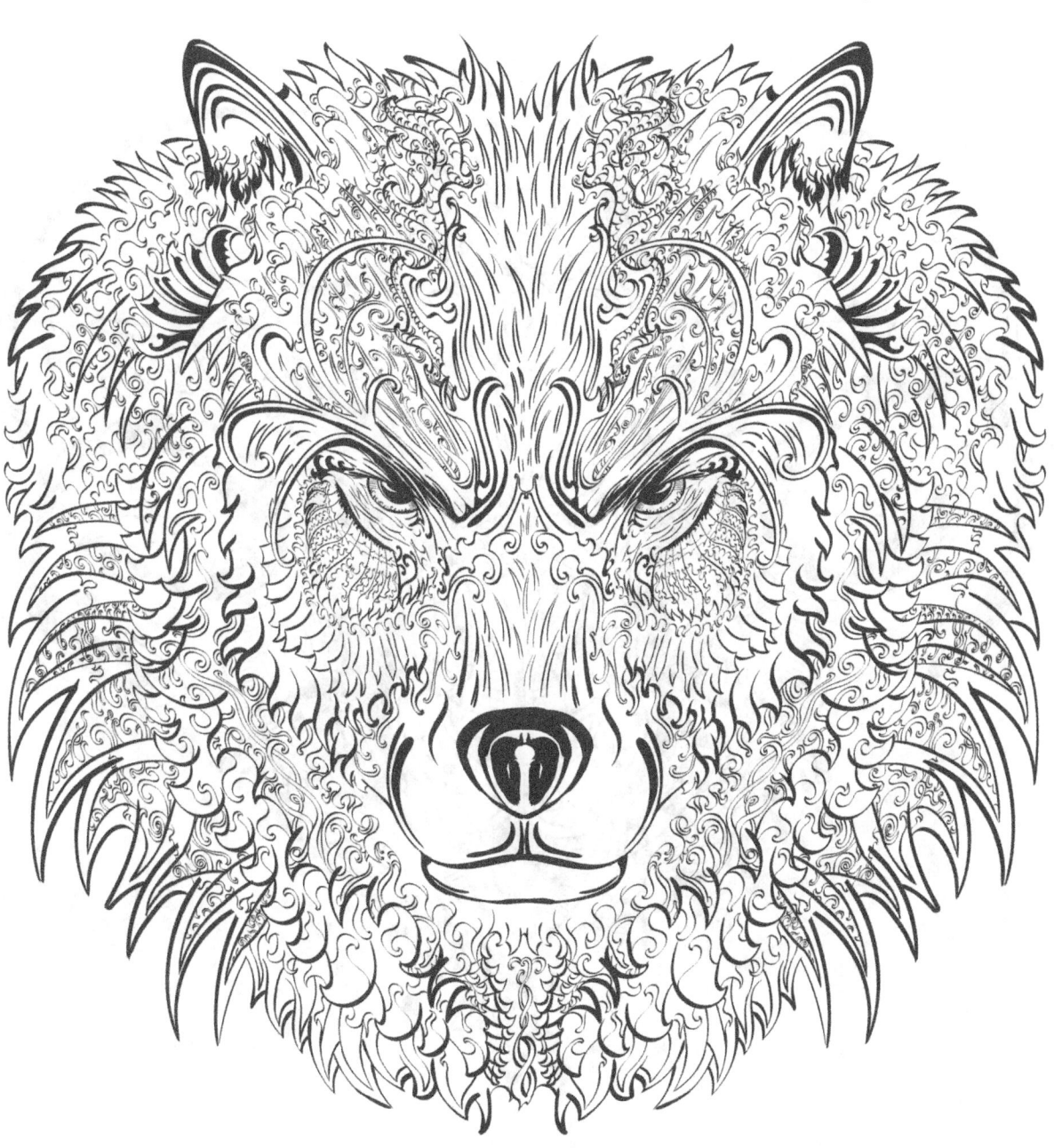

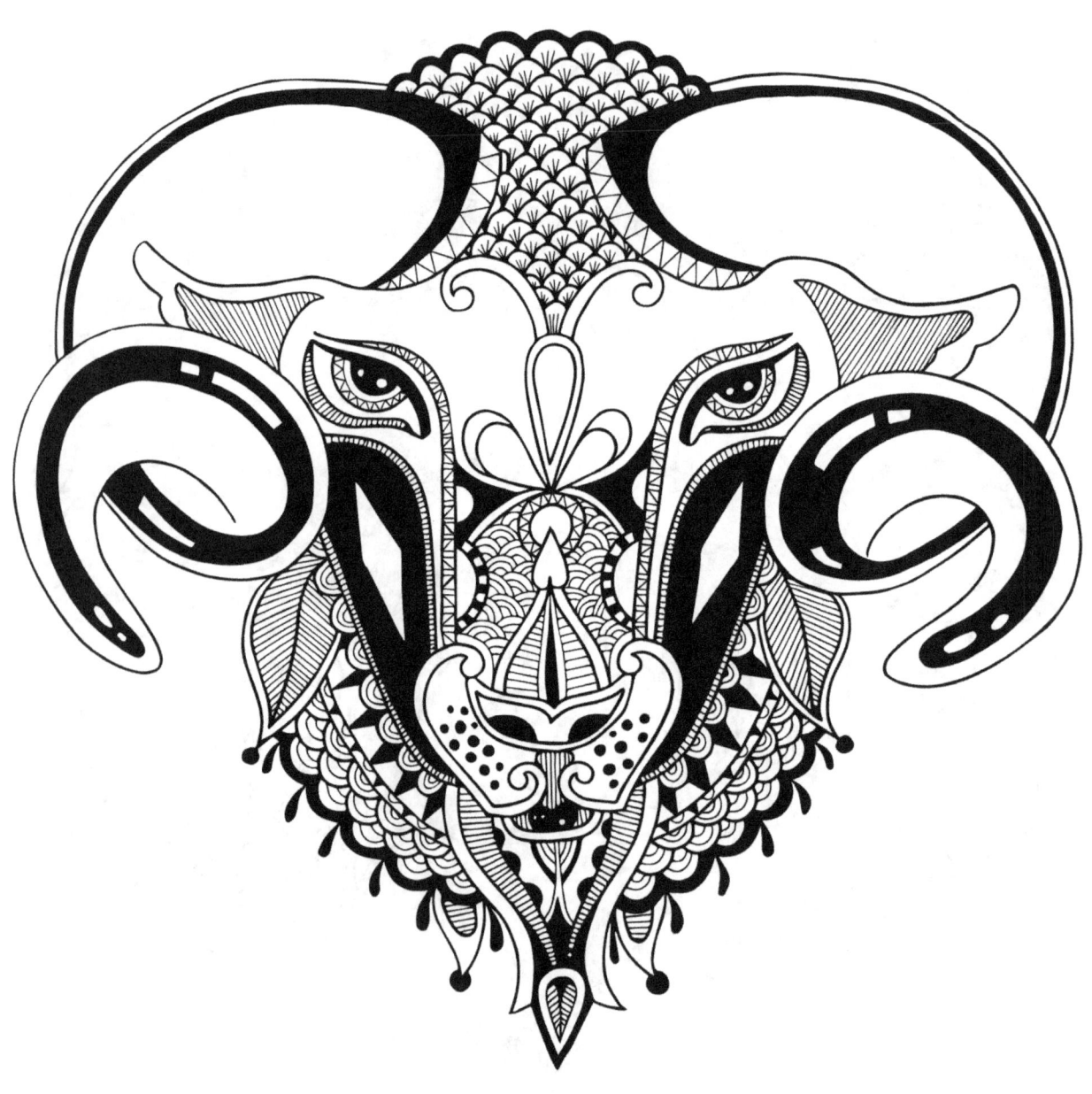

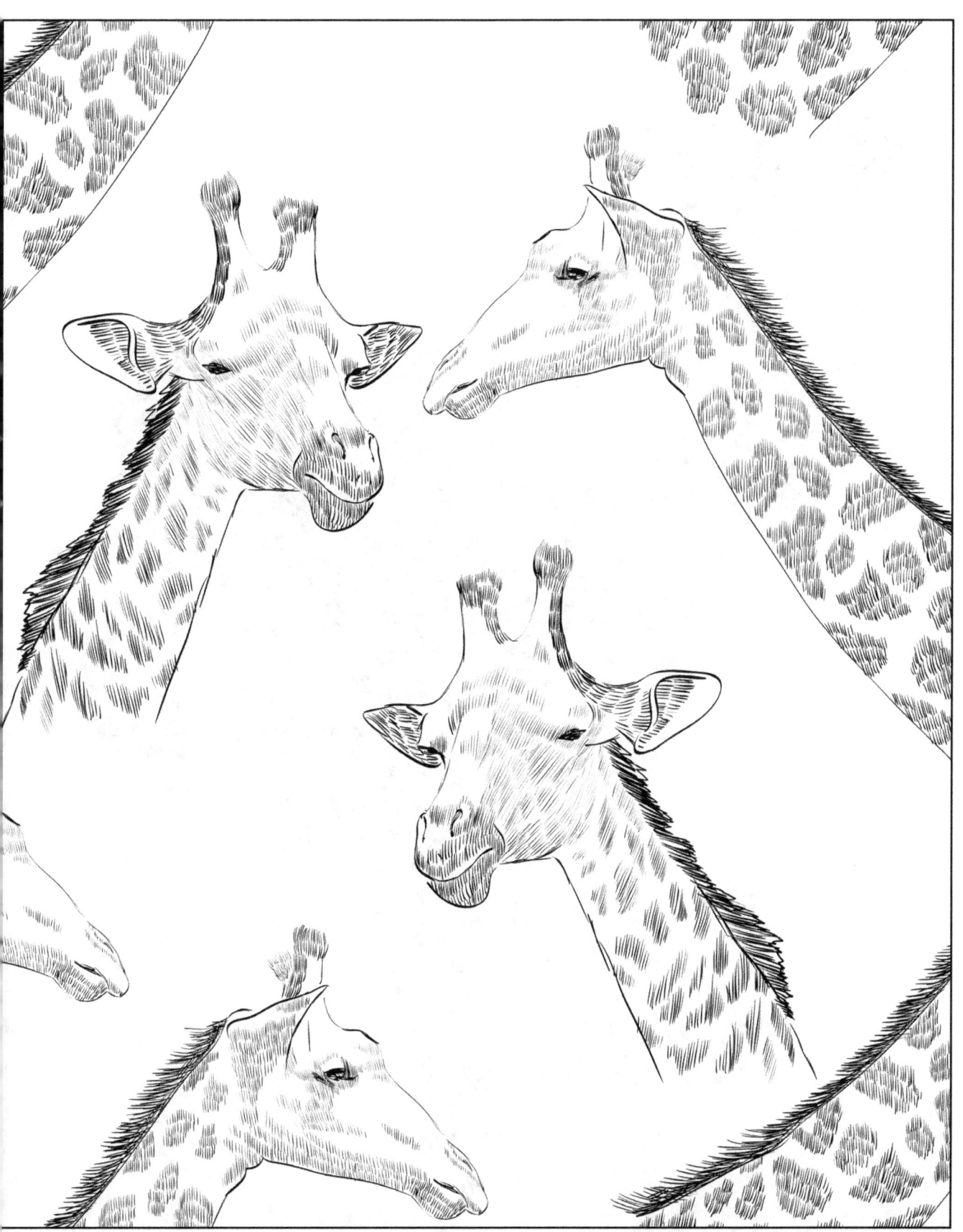

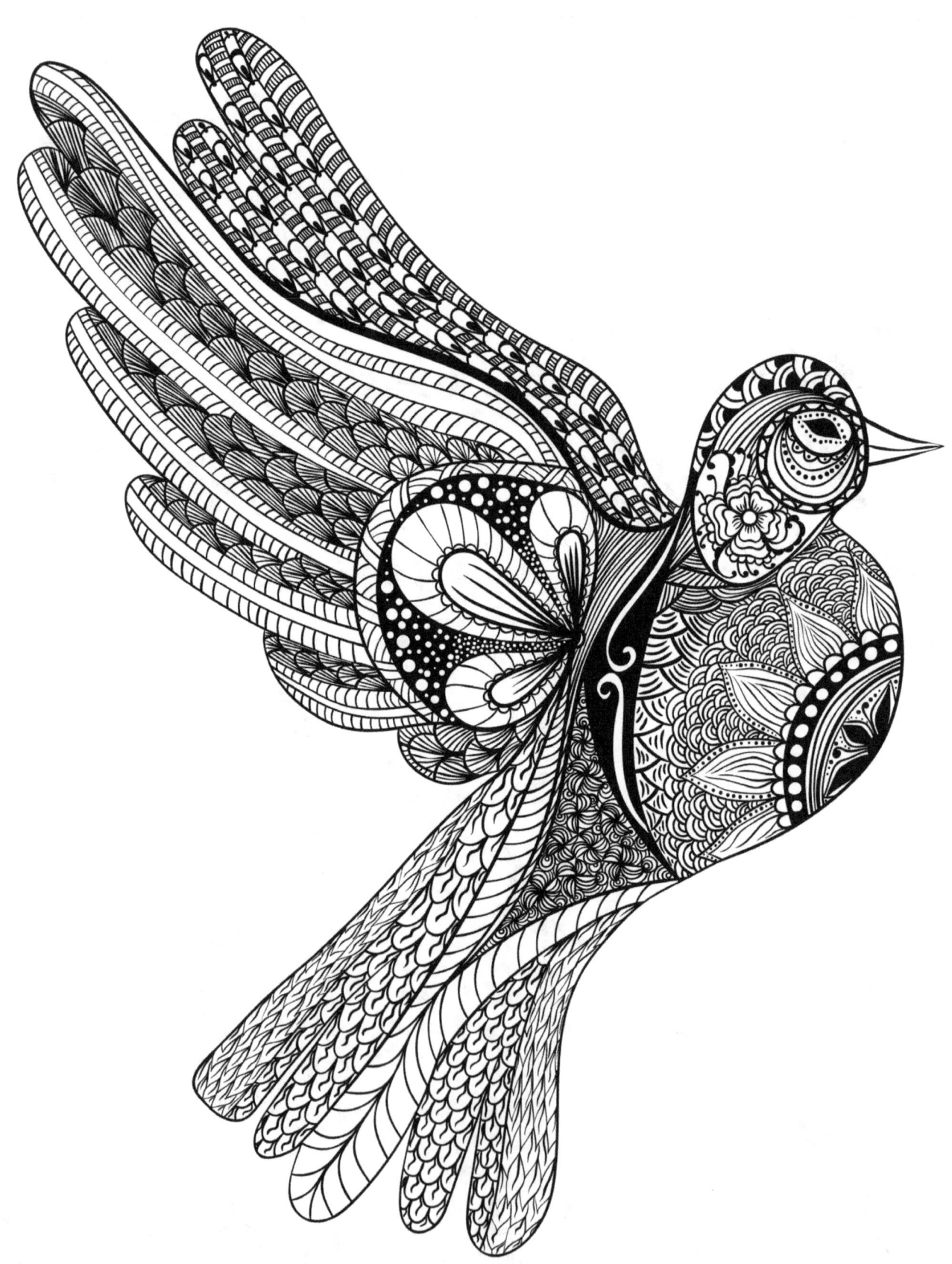

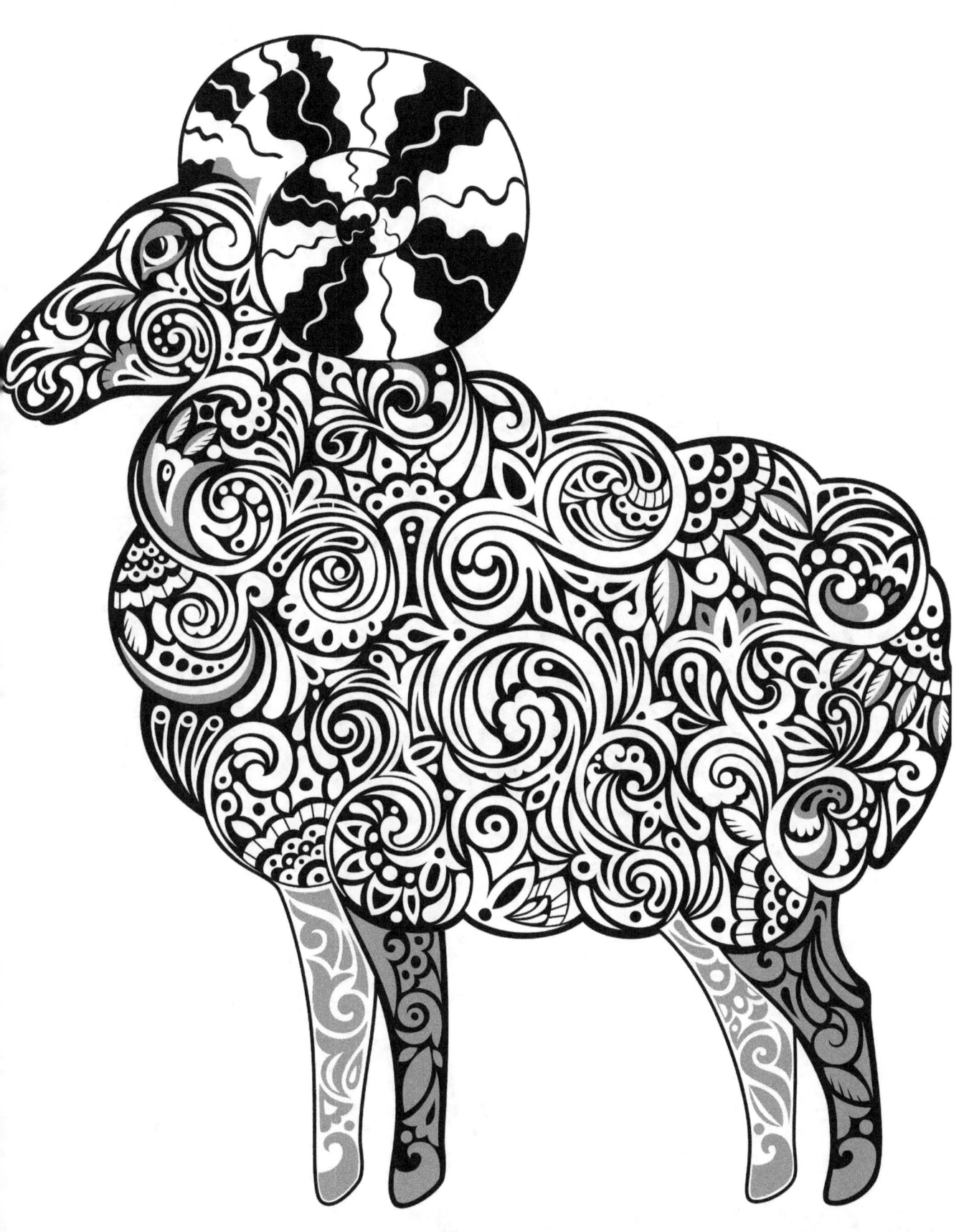

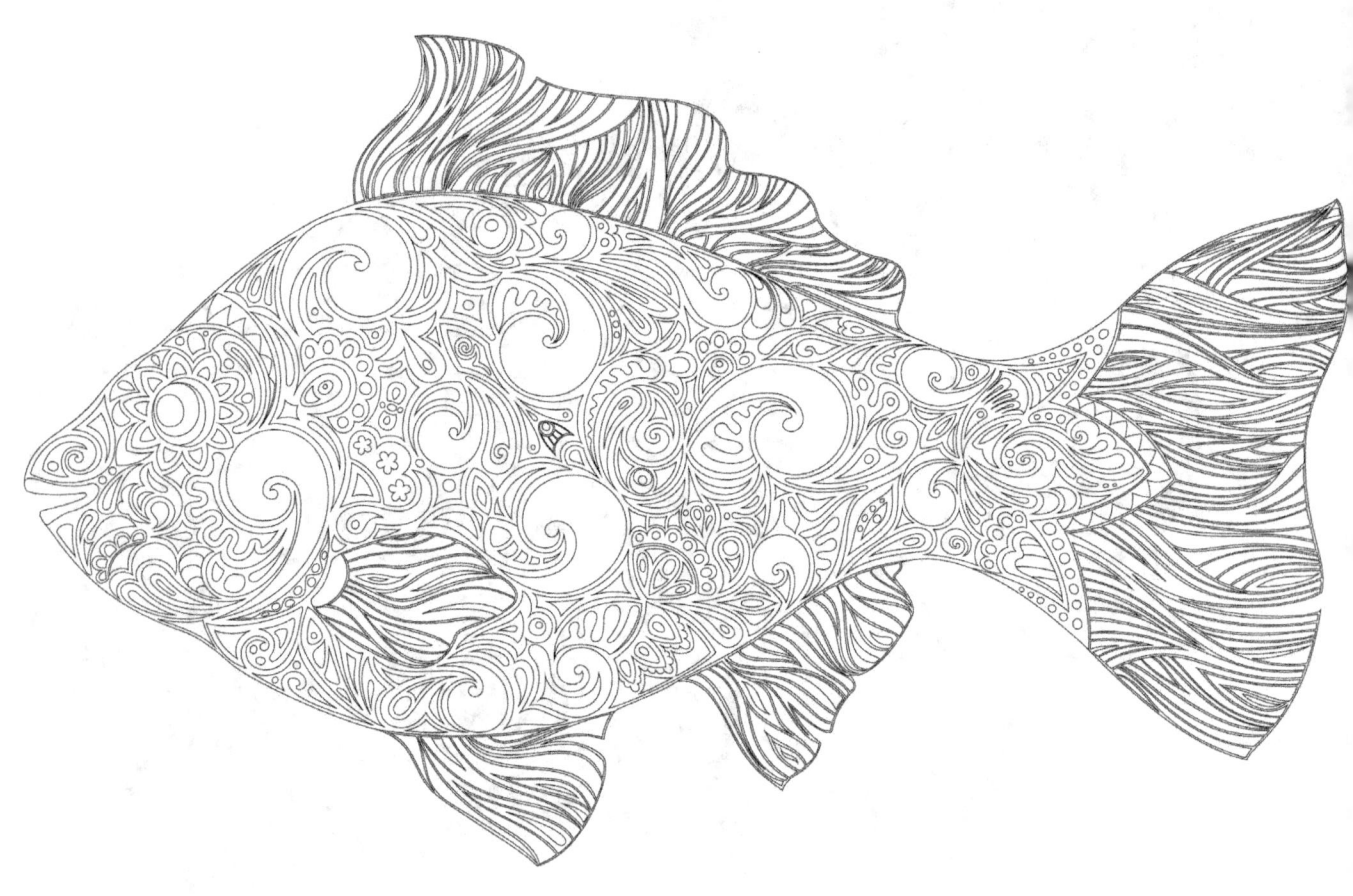

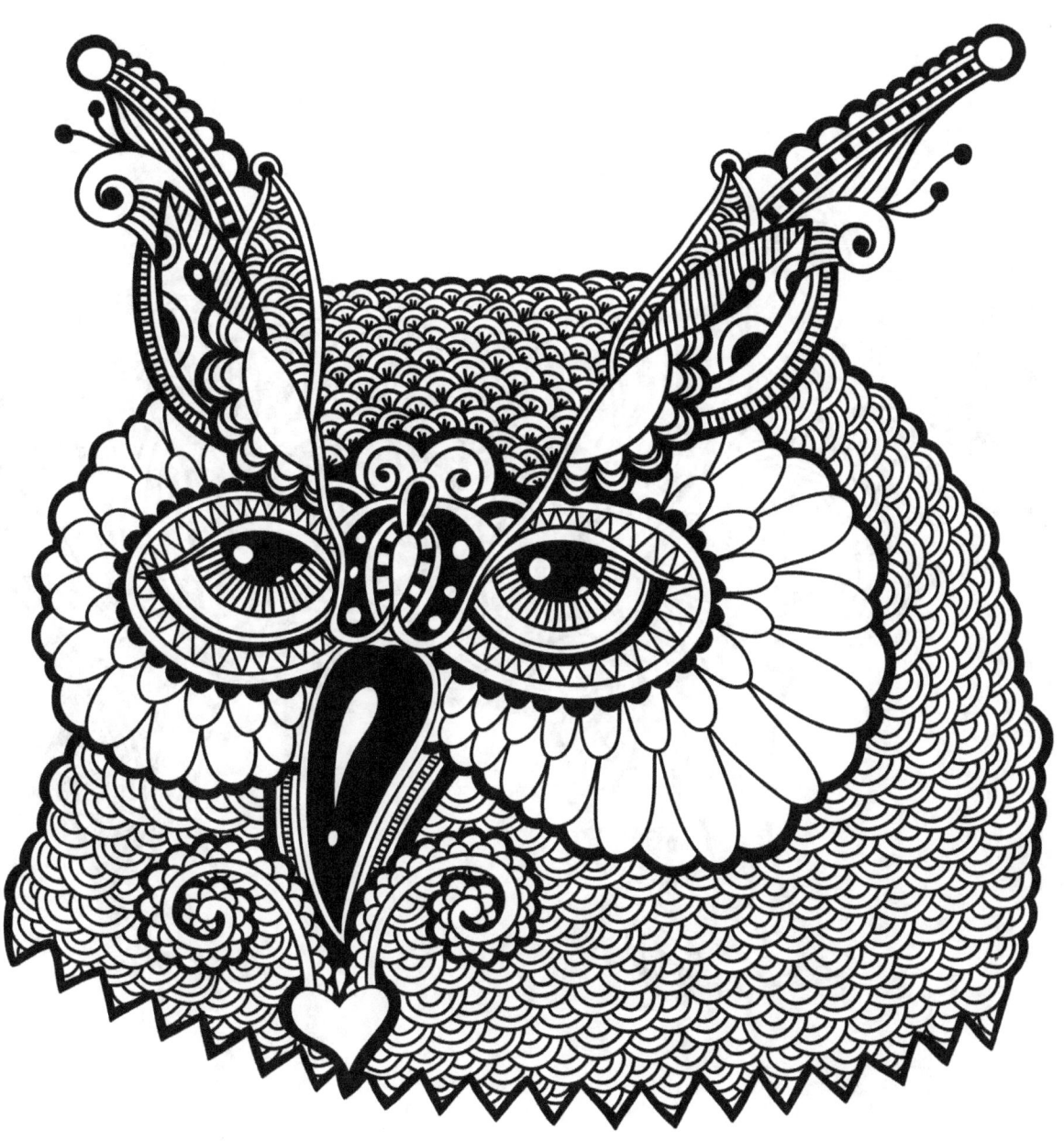

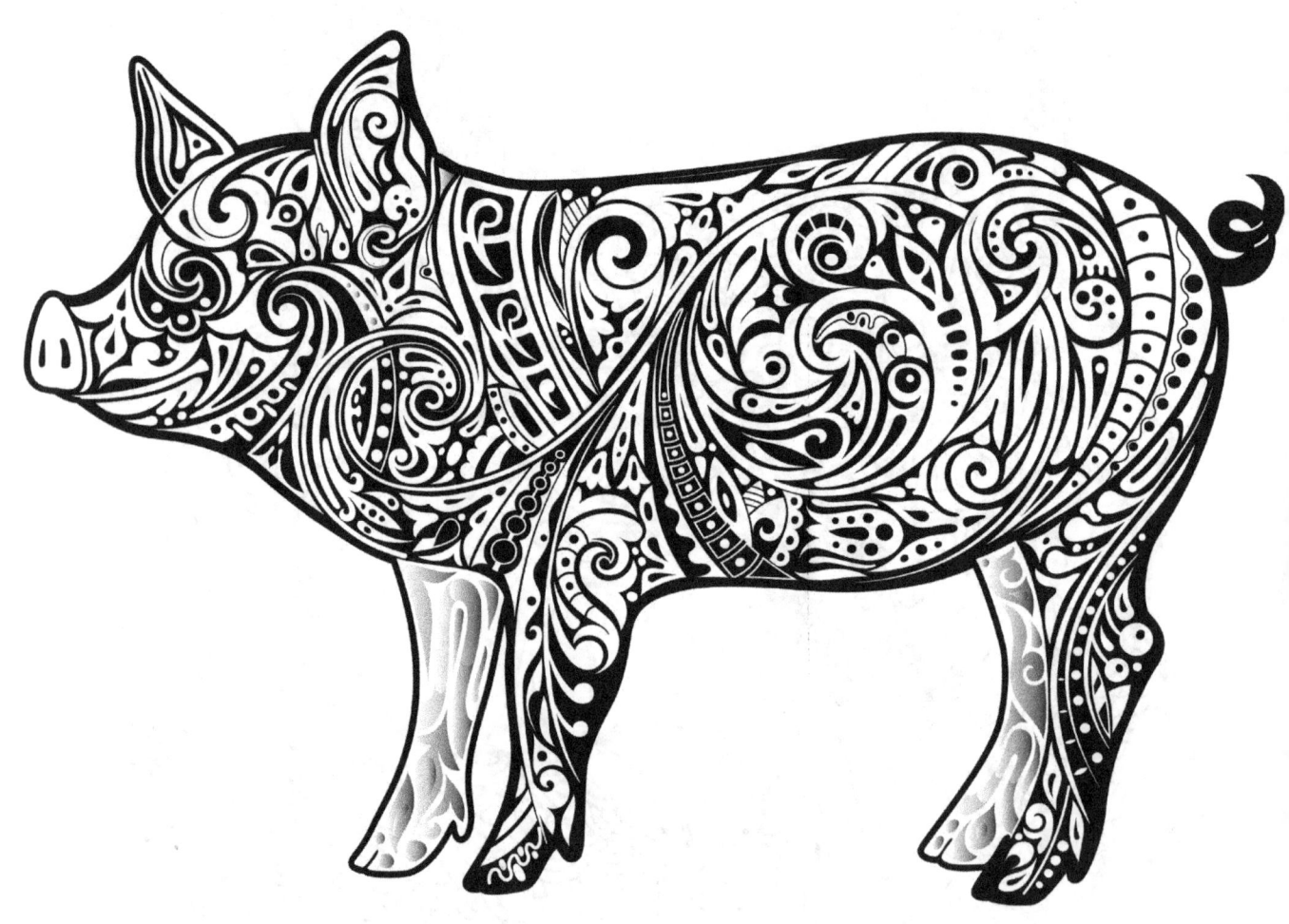

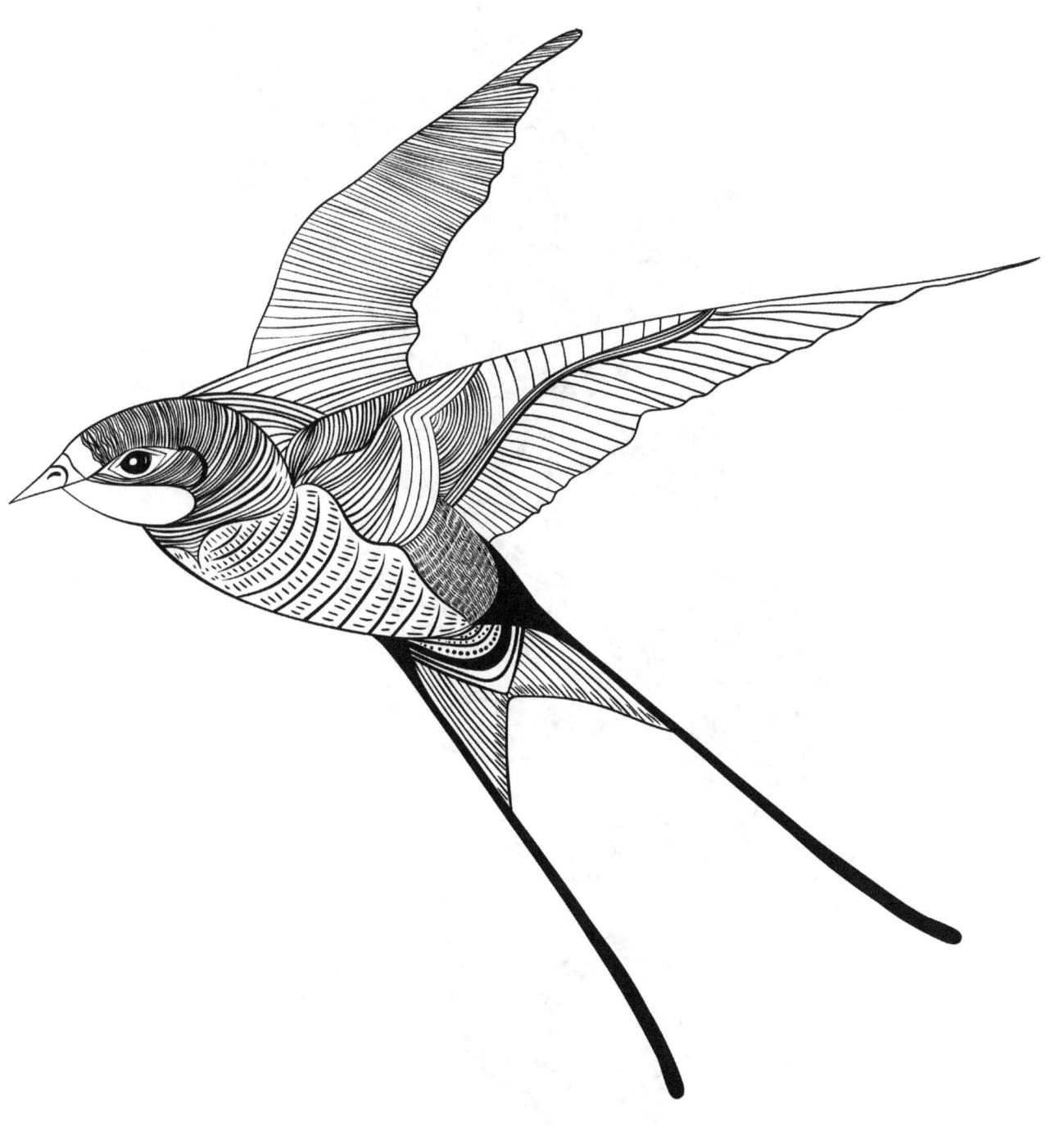

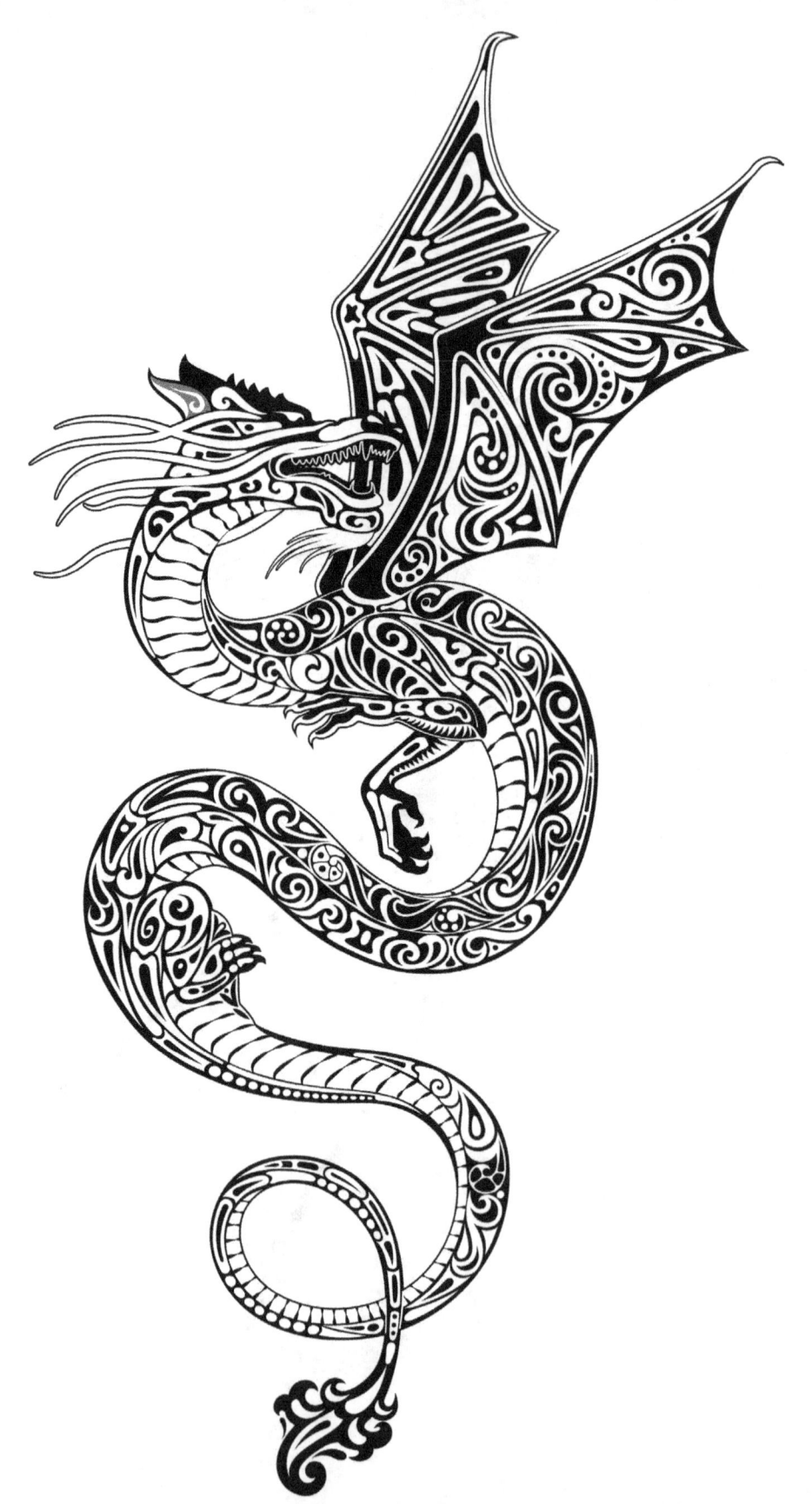

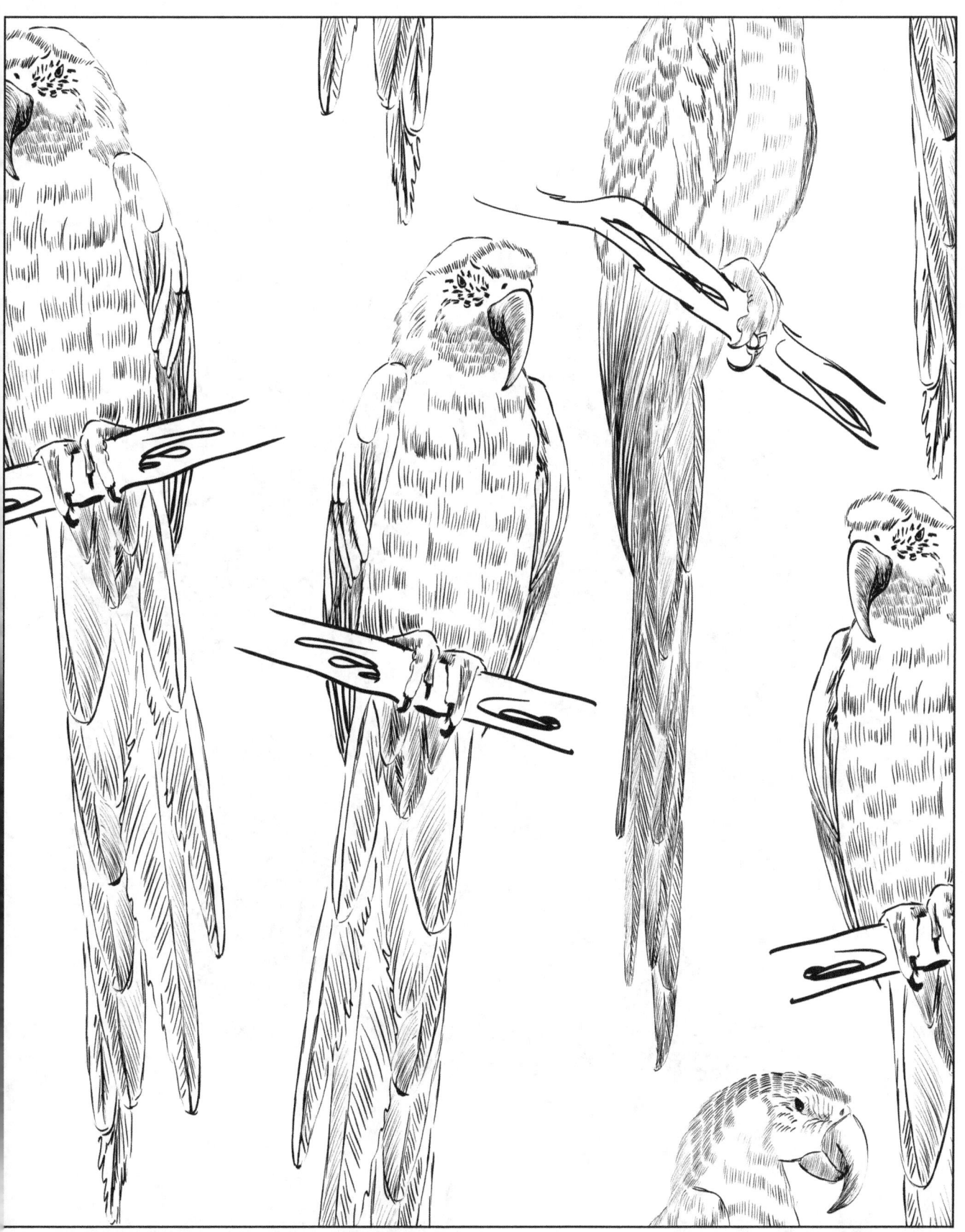

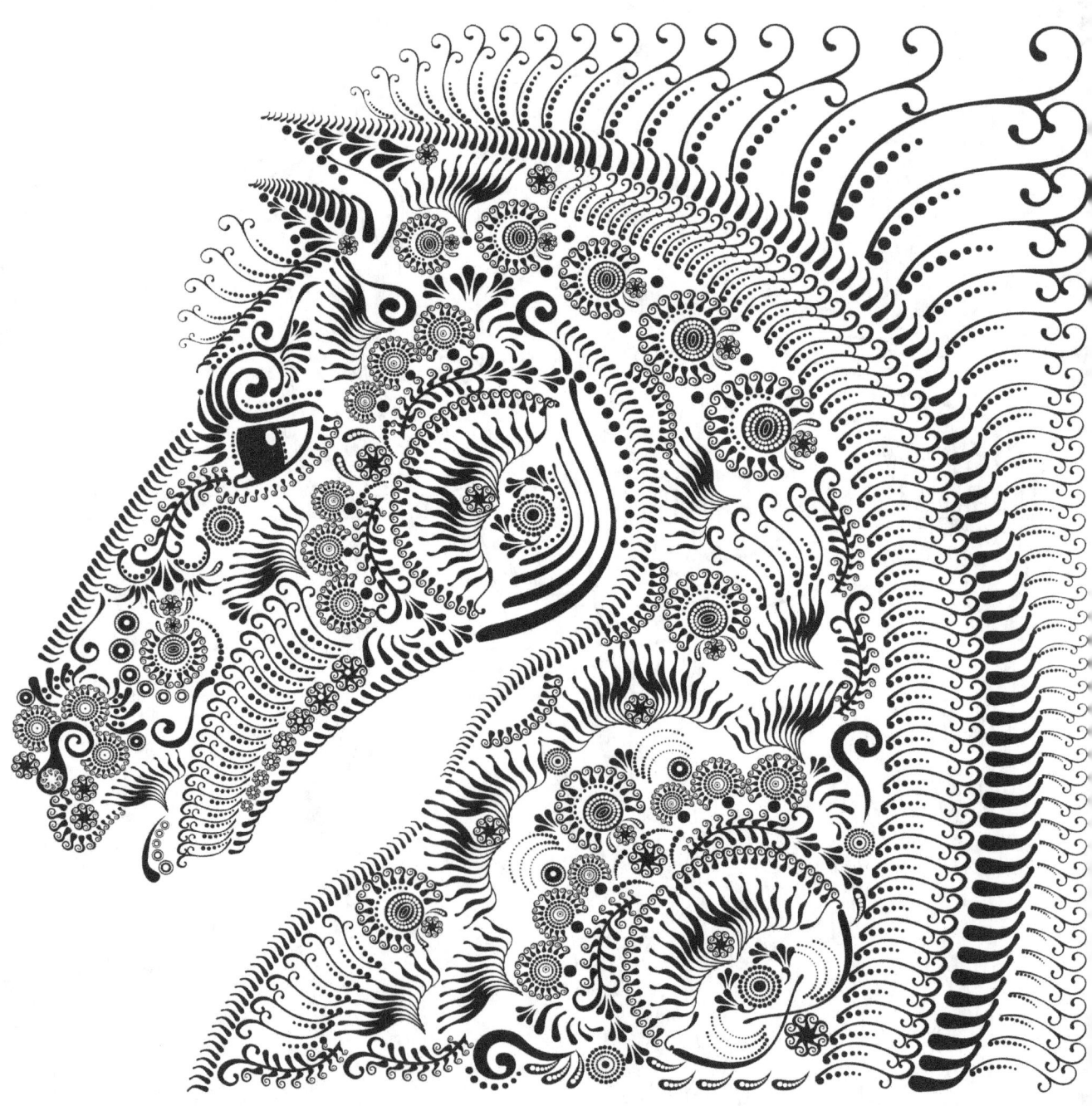

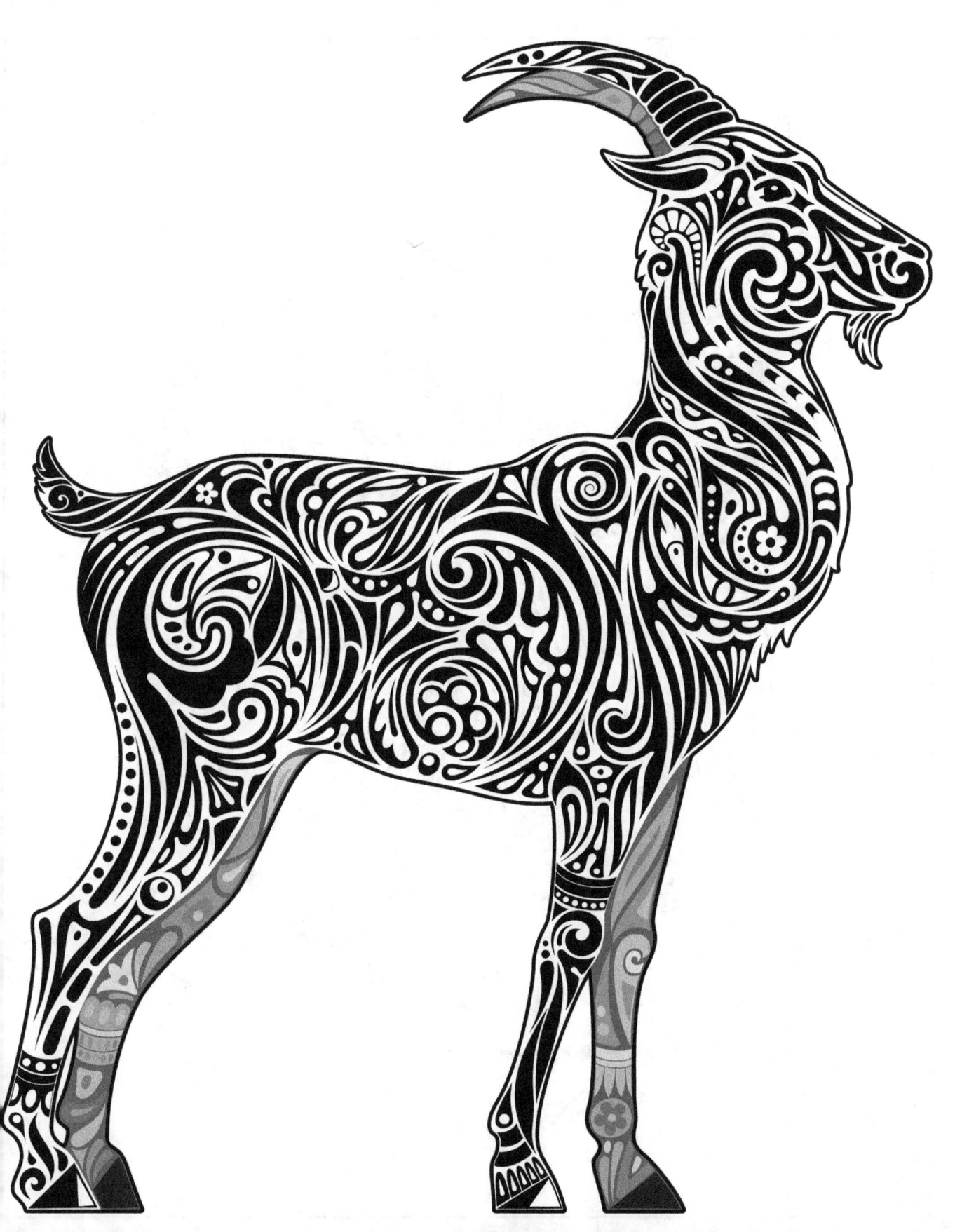

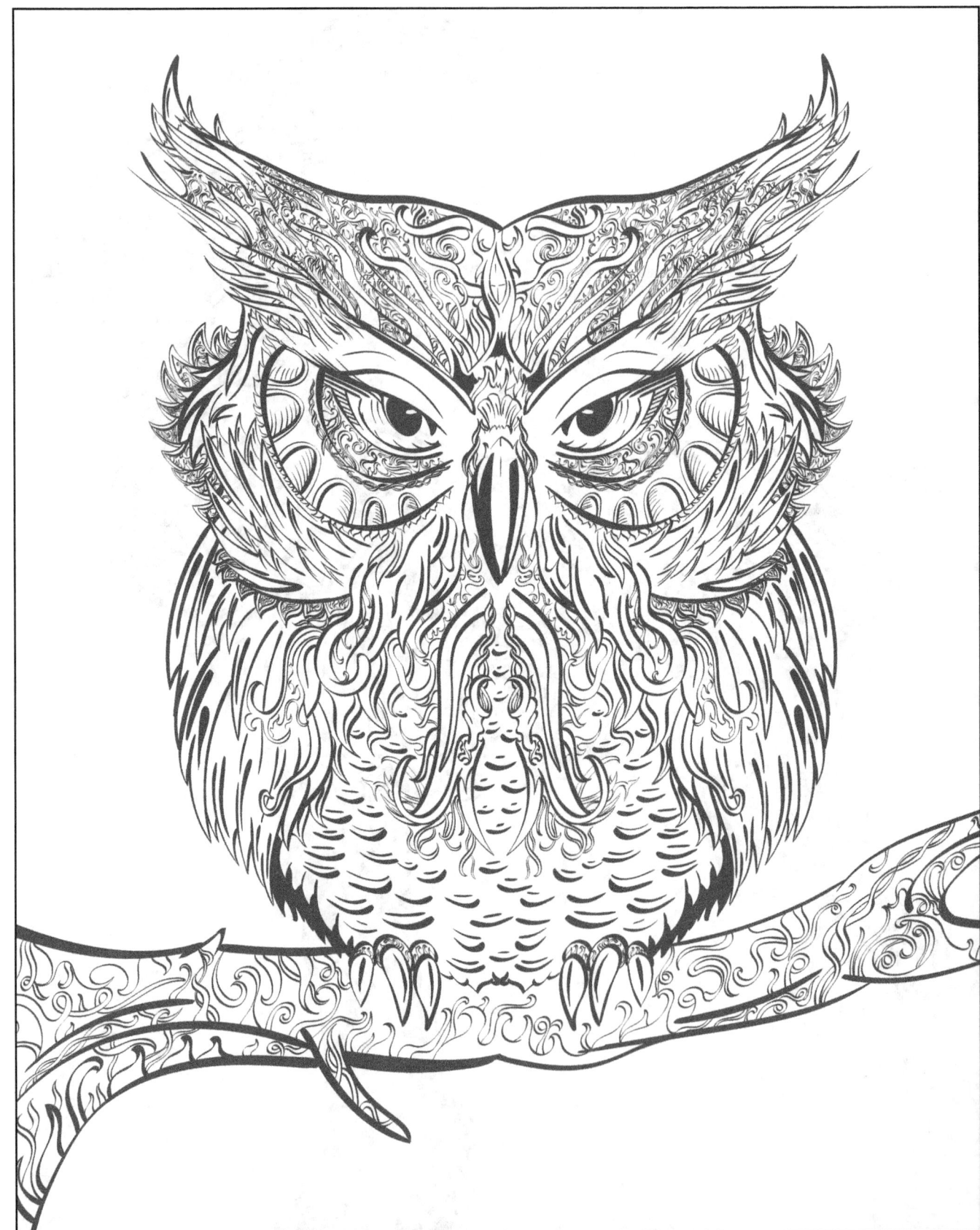

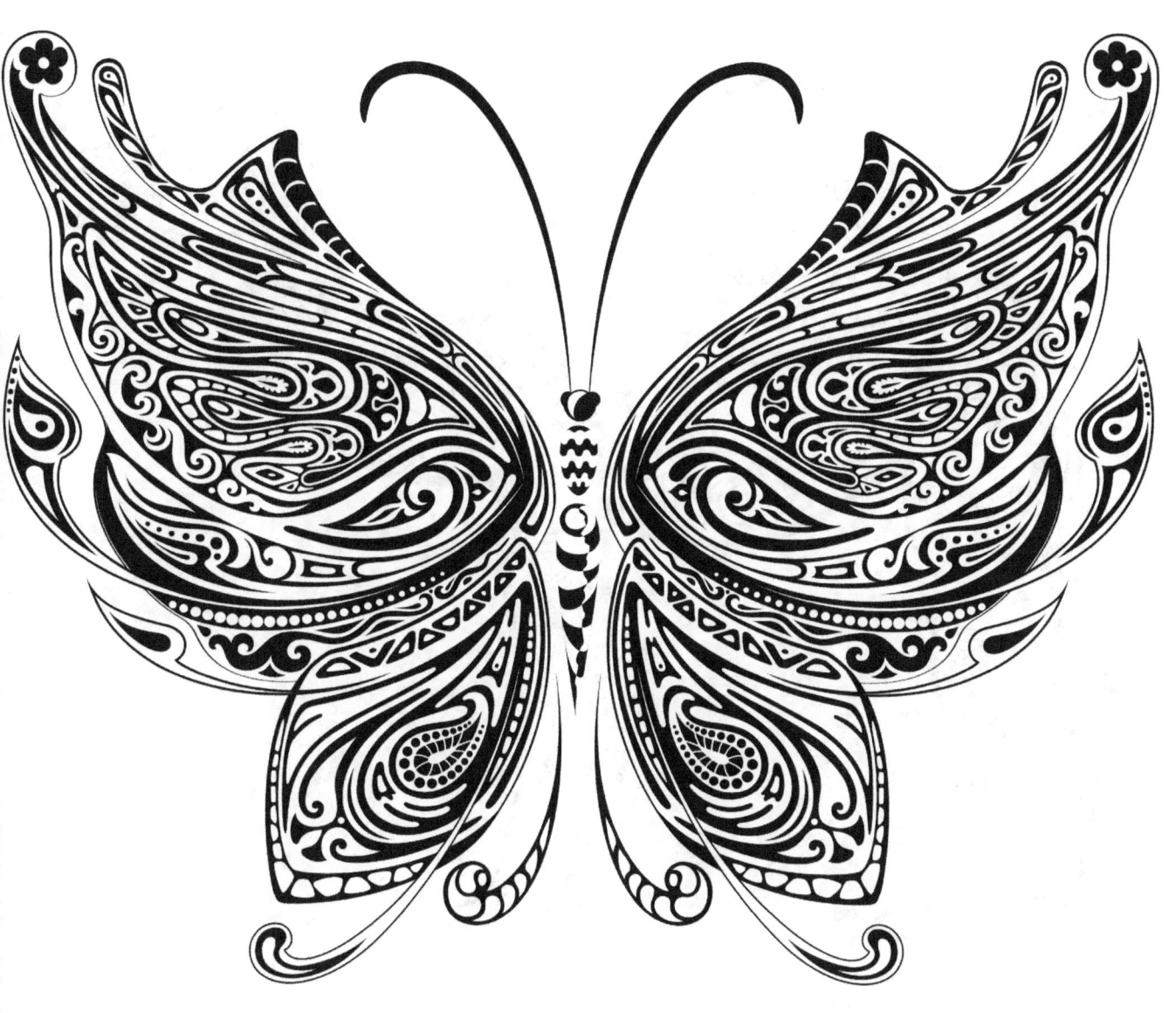

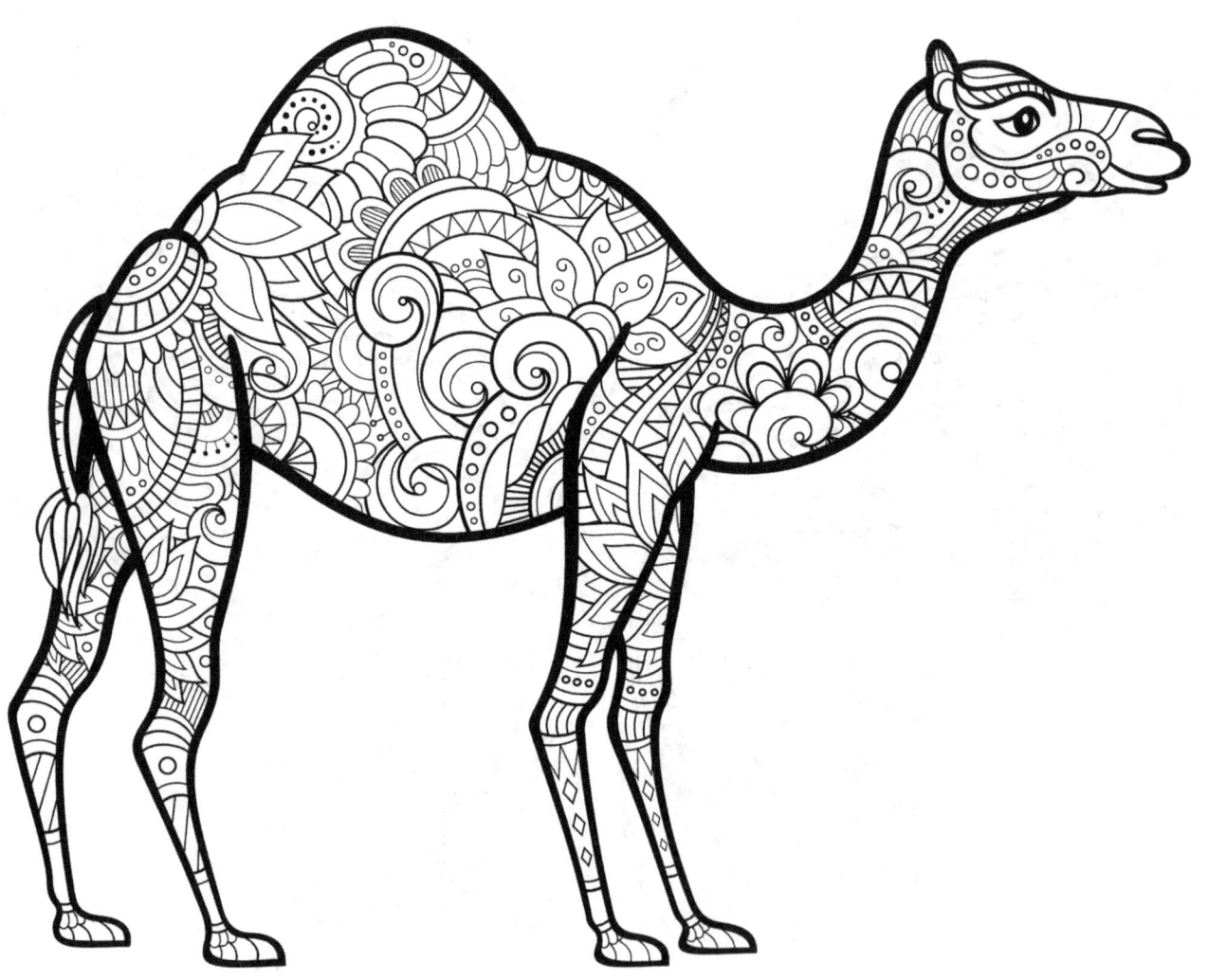

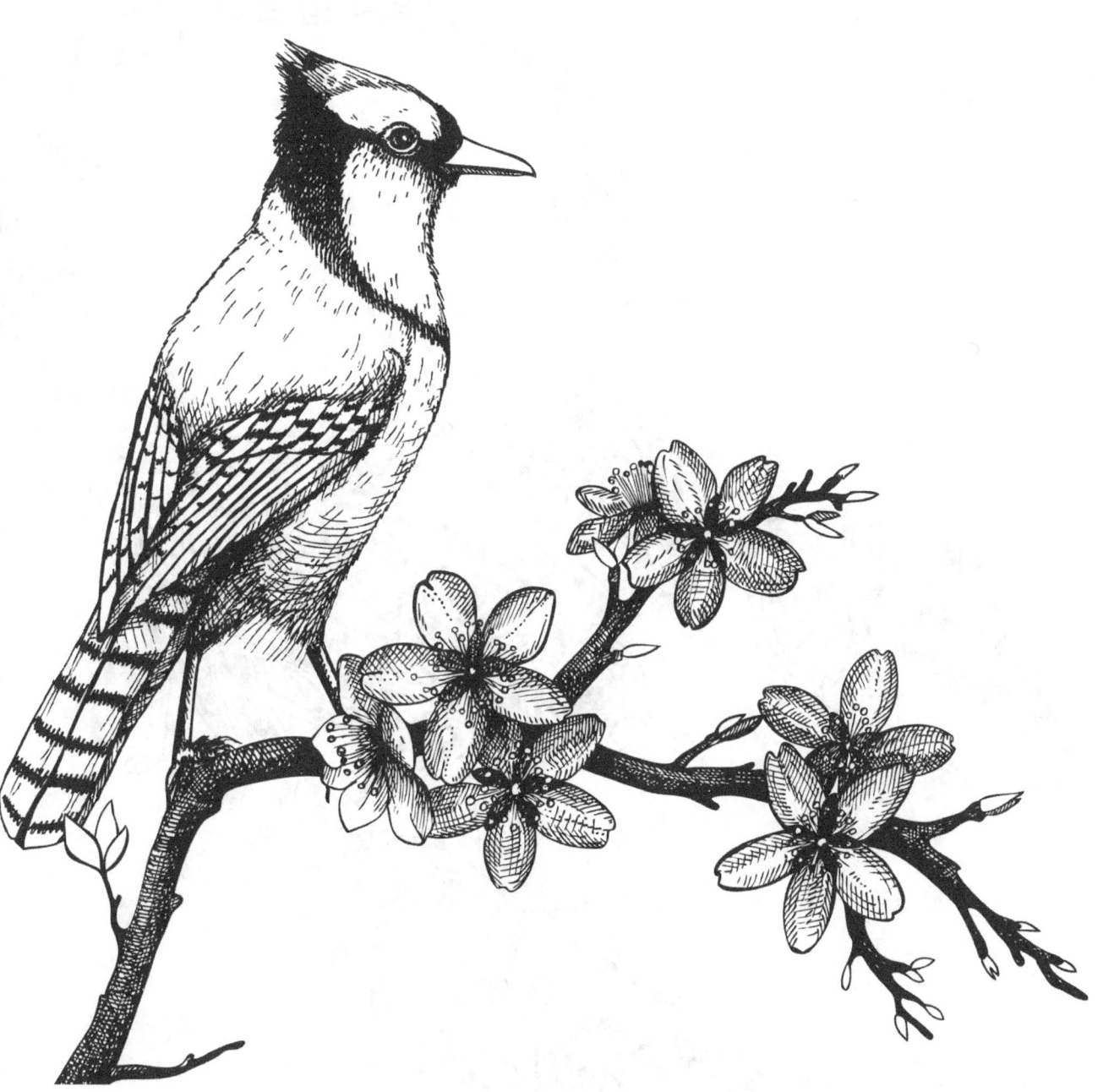

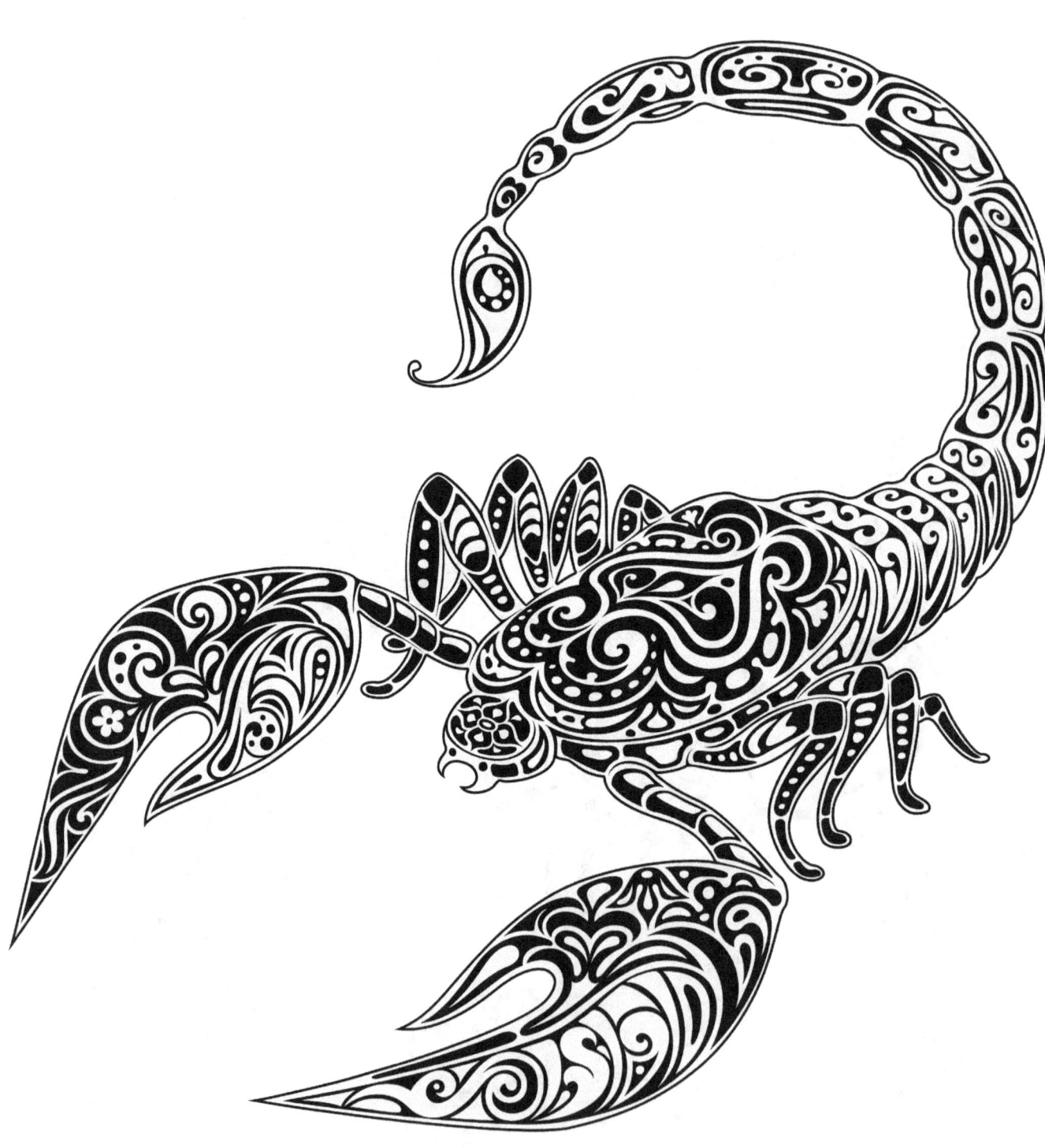

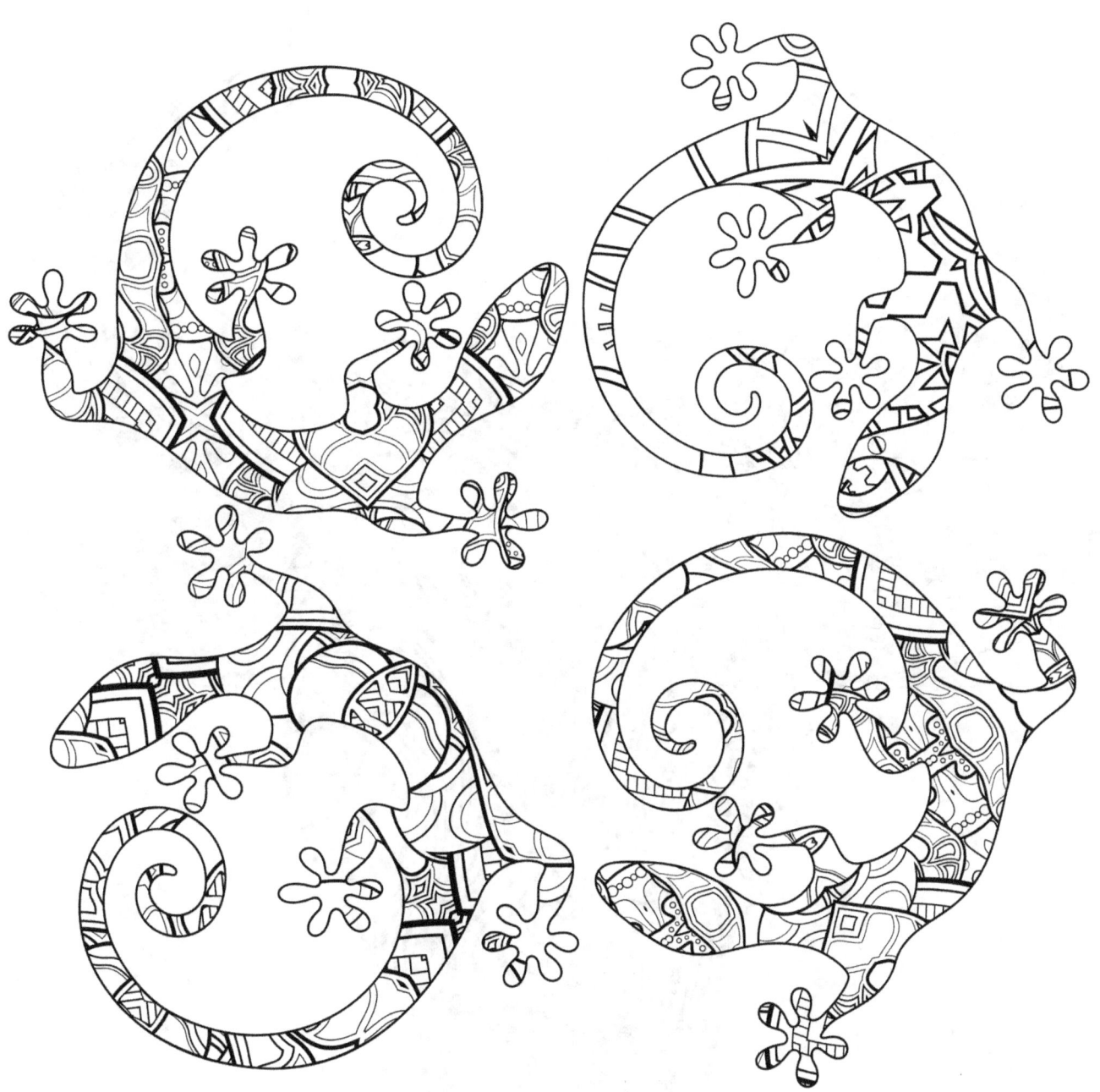

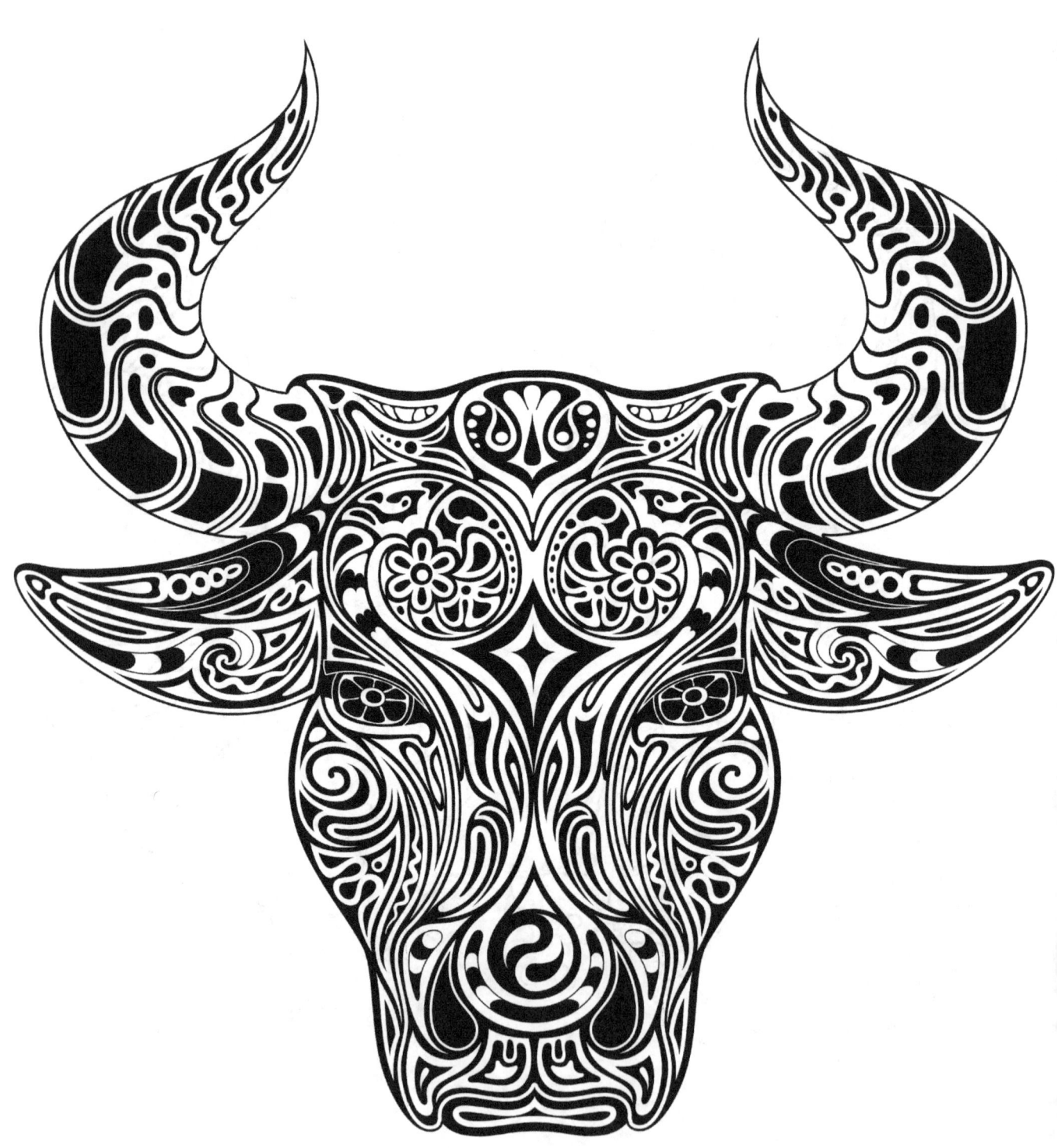

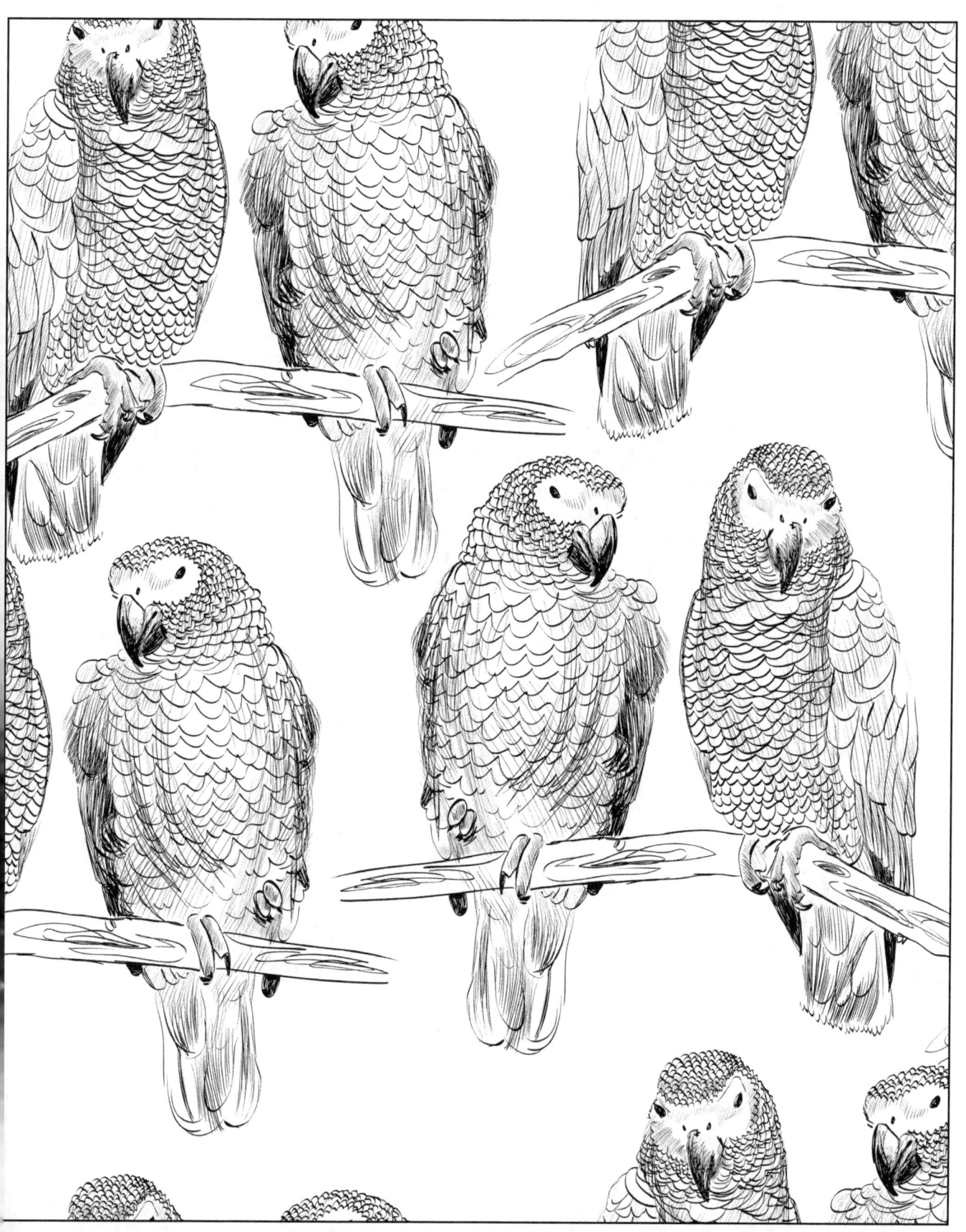

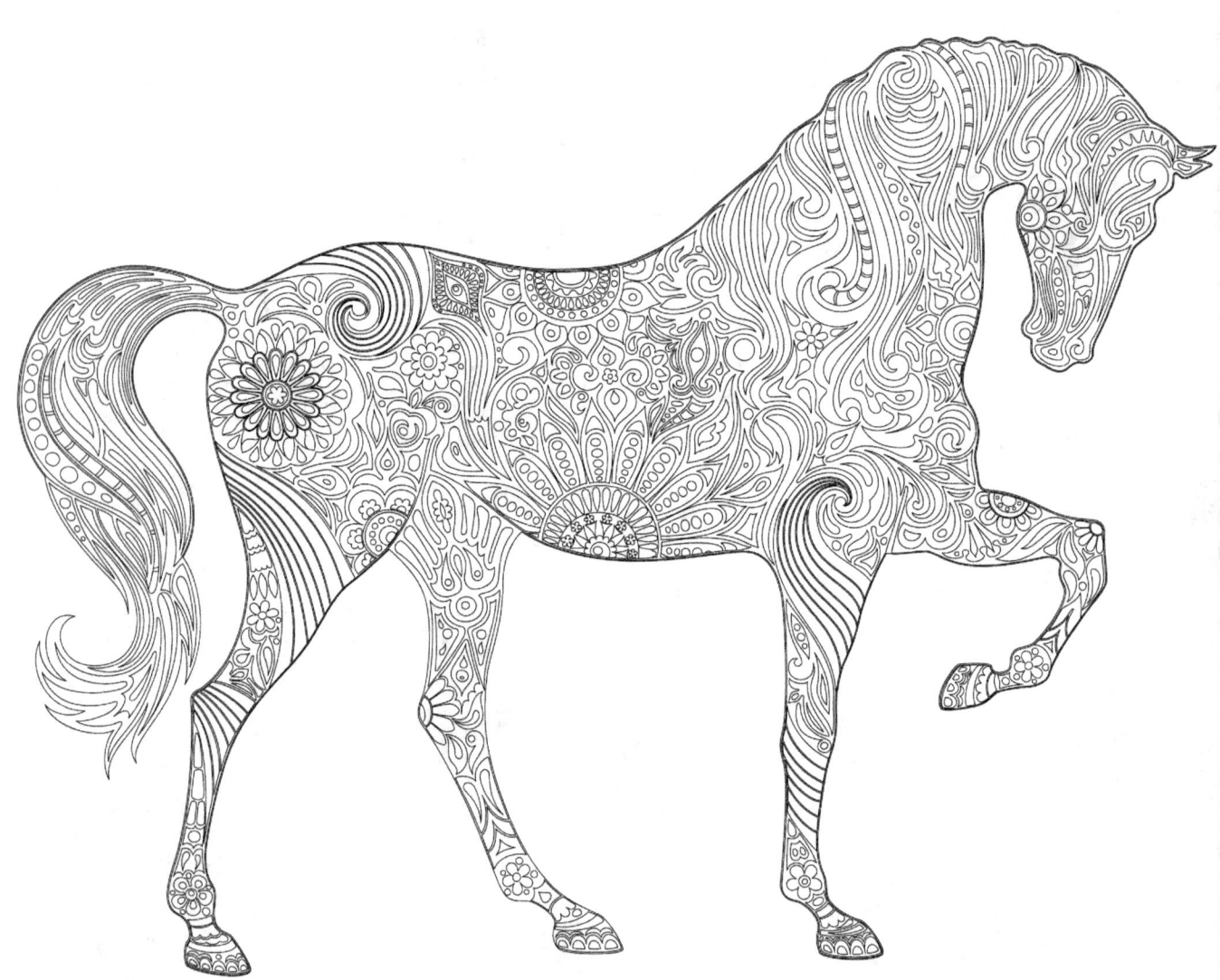

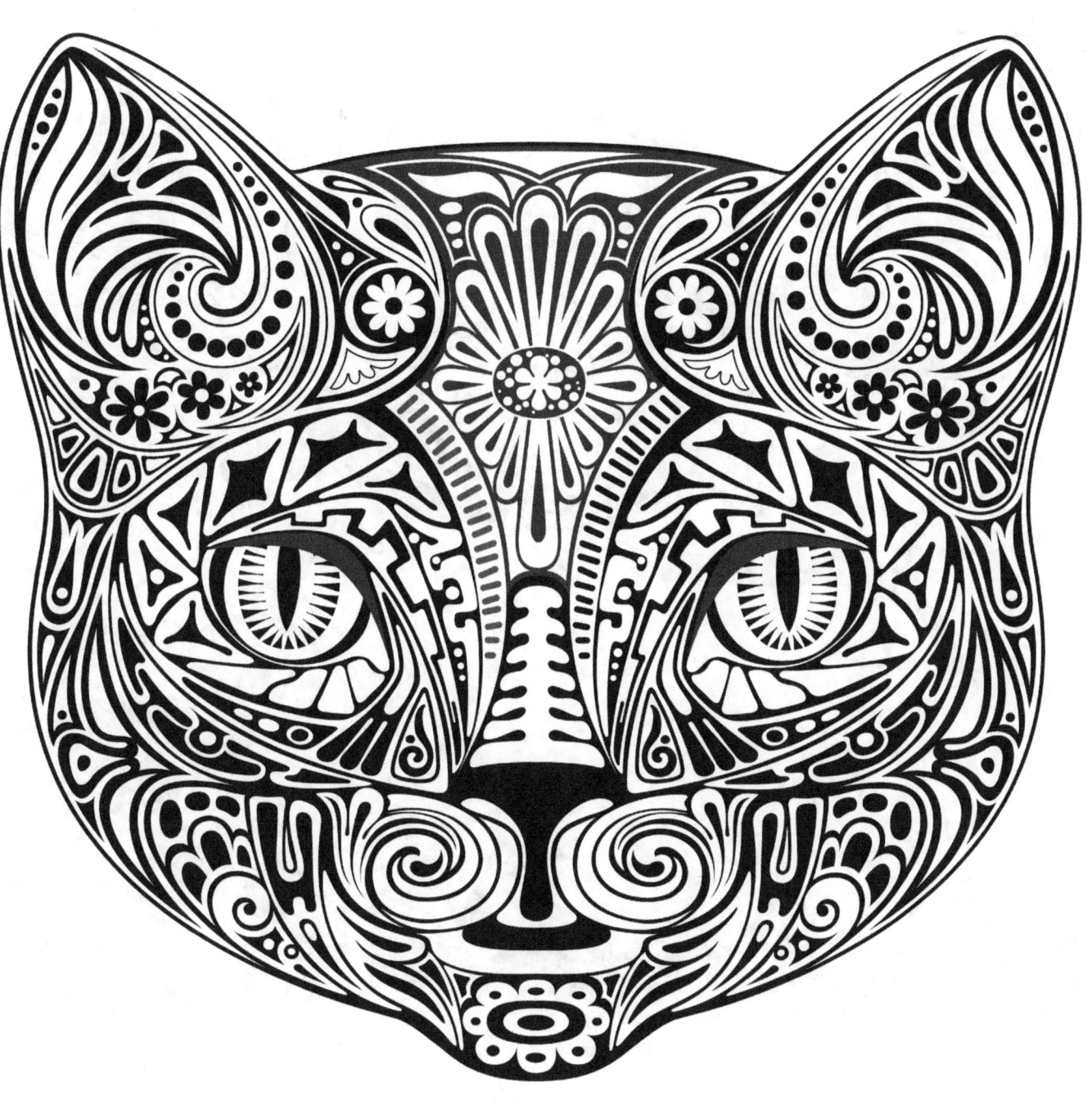

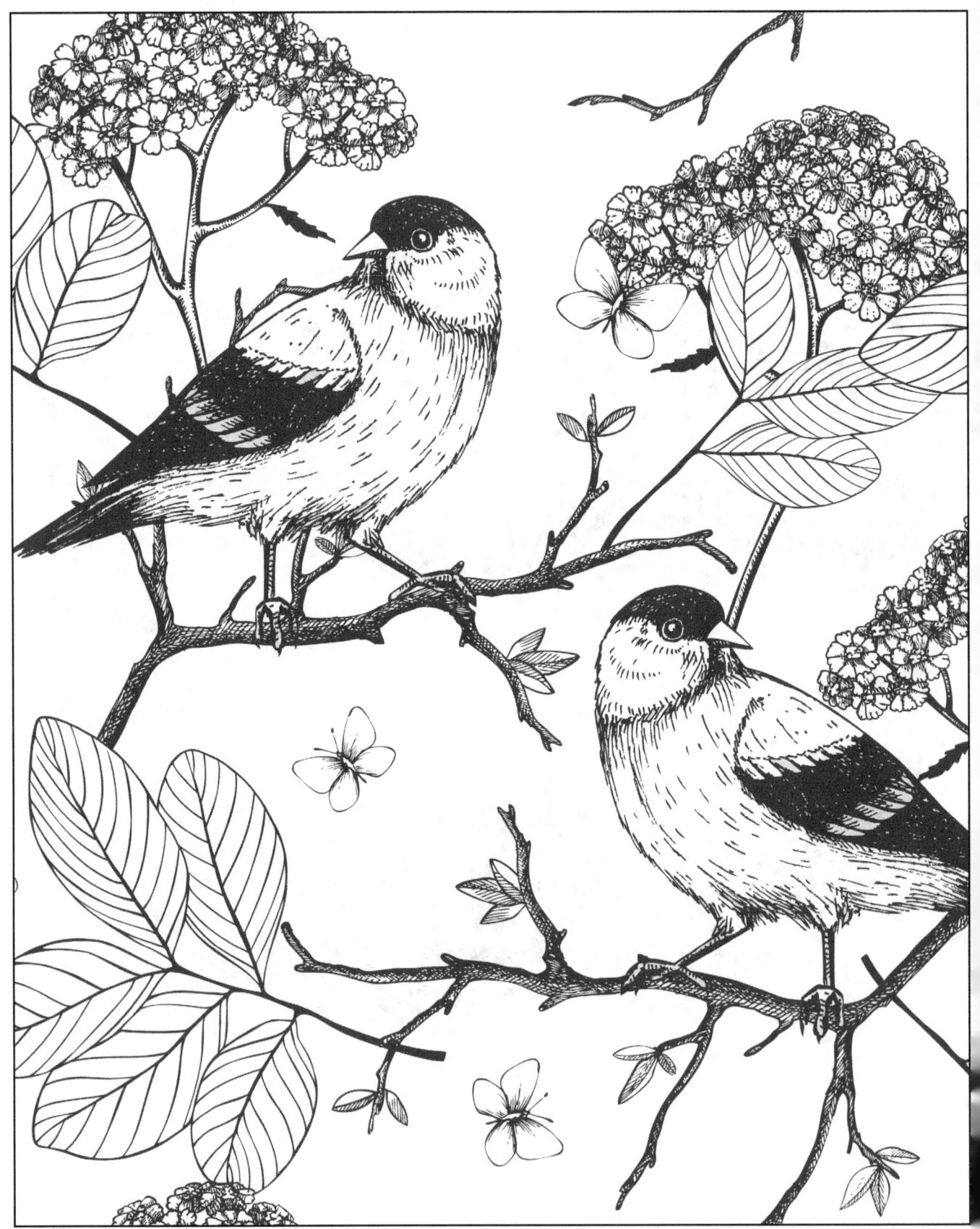

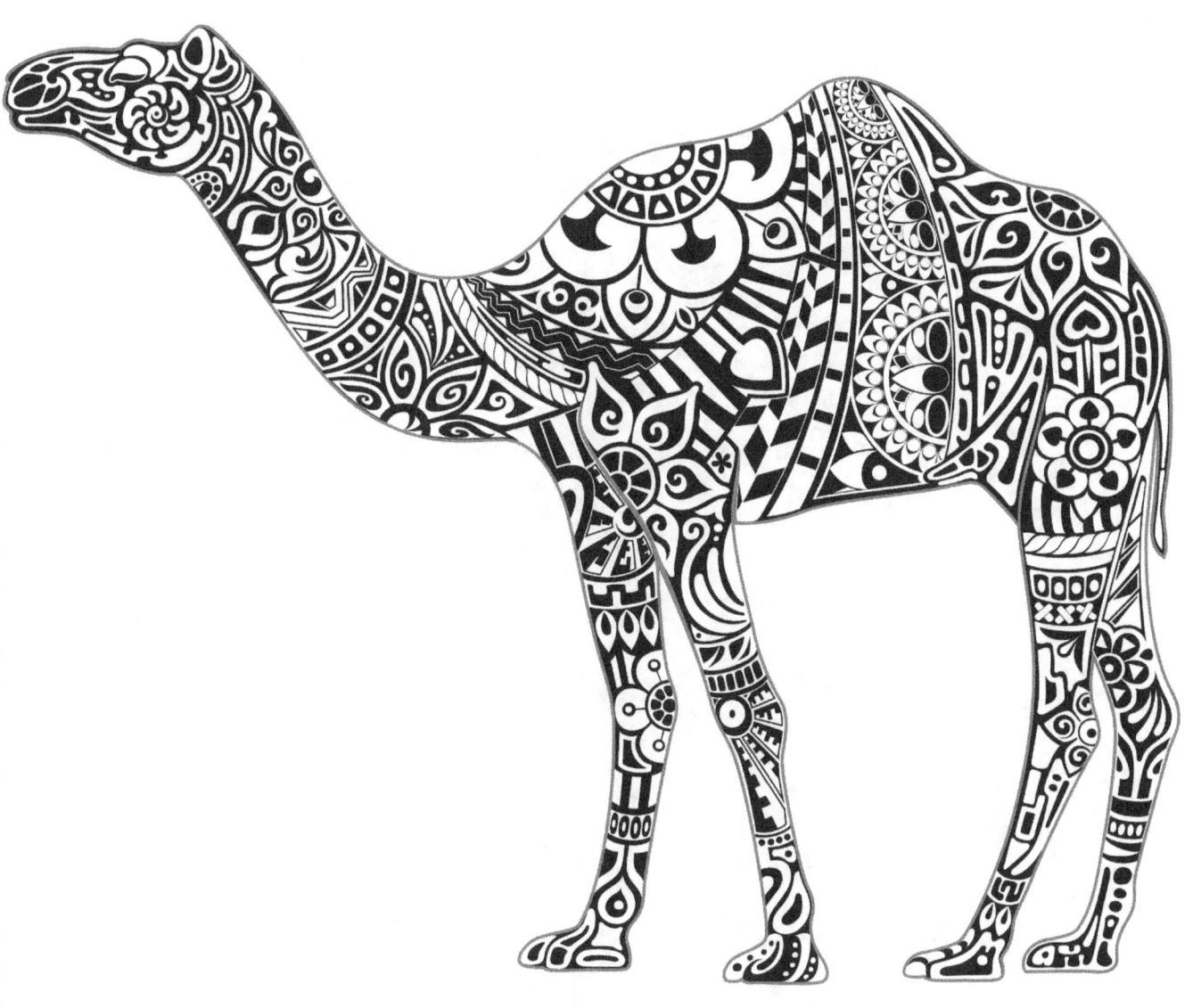

www.ingramcontent.com/pod-product-compliance
Lightning Source LLC
Chambersburg PA
CBHW081018170526
45158CB00010B/3093